THE
COMPLETE
IDIOT'S
GUIDE® TO

Selling Your Crafts

by Chris Franchetti Michaels

ALPHA

A member of Penguin Group (USA) Inc.

ALPHA BOOKS

Published by the Penguin Group

Penguin Group (USA) Inc., 375 Hudson Street, New York, New York 10014, USA

Penguin Group (Canada), 90 Eglinton Avenue East, Suite 700, Toronto, Ontario M4P 2Y3, Canada (a division of Pearson Penguin Canada Inc.)

Penguin Books Ltd., 80 Strand, London WC2R 0RL, England

Penguin Ireland, 25 St. Stephen's Green, Dublin 2, Ireland (a division of Penguin Books Ltd.)

Penguin Group (Australia), 250 Camberwell Road, Camberwell, Victoria 3124, Australia (a division of Pearson Australia Group Pty. Ltd.)

Penguin Books India Pvt. Ltd., 11 Community Centre, Panchsheel Park, New Delhi—110 017, India

Penguin Group (NZ), 67 Apollo Drive, Rosedale, North Shore, Auckland 1311, New Zealand (a division of Pearson New Zealand Ltd.)

Penguin Books (South Africa) (Pty.) Ltd., 24 Sturdee Avenue, Rosebank, Johannesburg 2196, South Africa

Penguin Books Ltd., Registered Offices: 80 Strand, London WC2R 0RL, England

Copyright © 2010 by Chris Franchetti Michaels

International Standard Book Number: 978-1-59257-991-4
Library of Congress Catalog Card Number: 2009943487

12 11 10   8 7 6 5 4 3 2 1

Interpretation of the printing code: The rightmost number of the first series of numbers is the year of the book's printing; the rightmost number of the second series of numbers is the number of the book's printing. For example, a printing code of 10-1 shows that the first printing occurred in 2010.

Printed in the United States of America

Note: This publication contains the opinions and ideas of its author. It is intended to provide helpful and informative material on the subject matter covered. It is sold with the understanding that the author and publisher are not engaged in rendering professional services in the book. If the reader requires personal assistance or advice, a competent professional should be consulted.

The author and publisher specifically disclaim any responsibility for any liability, loss, or risk, personal or otherwise, which is incurred as a consequence, directly or indirectly, of the use and application of any of the contents of this book.

Most Alpha books are available at special quantity discounts for bulk purchases for sales promotions, premiums, fund-raising, or educational use. Special books, or book excerpts, can also be created to fit specific needs.

For details, write: Special Markets, Alpha Books, 375 Hudson Street, New York, NY 10014.

Publisher: *Marie Butler-Knight*
Associate Publisher: *Mike Sanders*
Senior Managing Editor: *Billy Fields*
Acquisitions Editors: *Karyn Gerhardt, Randy Ladenheim-Gil*
Development Editor: *Jennifer Bowles*
Senior Production Editor: *Janette Lynn*

Copy Editor: *Lisanne Jensen*
Cover Designer: *Kurt Owens*
Book Designer: *Trina Wurst*
Indexer: *Julie Bess*
Layout: *Brian Massey*
Proofreader: *Laura Caddell*

Contents at a Glance

Contents

Introduction

Craft selling differs quite a bit from other selling ventures. Instead of merely searching for premade merchandise and offering it for sale, you serve as both the creative mind and the source of skilled labor that bring your products into existence.

Why is that significant? It affects all the decisions you need to make as a seller, from pricing your wares to selecting the right sales venues to devising customer service polices. It also means that your selling goals may be very different from those of a typical businessperson.

This book is unlike most introductory business books because it focuses on your unique situation as a crafter. I won't tell you how to outsource your designs to workers in another country, apply for investment funding, or become a corporation. Instead, I'll show you a practical approach for getting started selling online or in person while you take some time to decide just how serious you wish to become.

How This Book Is Organized

The Complete Idiot's Guide to Selling Your Crafts is divided into the following five parts:

Part 1, "First Things First": This part is where I'll help you decide whether it's the right time to start selling. I'll also explain how and where you can sell your crafts and how to get your ducks in a row before you start.

Part 2, "Getting Started as a Casual Seller": The chapters in this part show you how to evolve from a pure hobbyist into a low-key, casual craft seller. You'll learn how to establish an inventory, set prices, adopt a marketing style, function as a seller, and promote your crafts.

Part 3, "Sales Venues for the Casual Seller and Beyond": At this point, you'll be ready to decide exactly how and where you'd like to begin offering your crafts for sale. We'll examine some of the most popular types of sales venues for beginners and more active sellers alike.

Part 4, "Transitioning into a More Active Seller": When you're ready to get more serious about selling, this part will guide you through the changes you need to make.

Part 5, "Sales Venues for the More Active Seller": Here's where we'll cover the traditional places where you can sell your crafts as a more serious seller. I'll explain the basics of setting up an e-commerce website, getting involved with craft shows, and finding wholesale accounts.

Tips, Tricks, Definitions, and Warnings

As you read each chapter, you'll occasionally notice a box containing extra information that's not covered in the regular text. This is where I tap you on the shoulder and make a suggestion or explain something important about what we're covering.

Here are the four types of boxes you'll encounter:

Term Tag

Read this box for a more complete definition of an italicized term in the text.

Hitting a Snag

Common mistakes can unravel your plans pretty quickly. Learn how to avoid them.

Selling Secrets

These are special tips that only an experienced seller can offer. Save time and frustration by learning them now.

Bits and Pieces

These little gems of advice will help you meet your selling goals.

Acknowledgments

Thanks to my agent, Marilyn Allen, for her ongoing help and encouragement, and to senior acquisitions editor Karyn Gerhard for identifying the need for this book and inviting me to write it. Thanks also to the entire team at Alpha who worked hard to whip the book into shape, including our development editor, Jennifer Bowles; senior production editor, Janette Lynn; and copy editor Lisanne Jensen. I also thank my husband and (in this case) business and legal consultant,

Dennis Michaels, for his advice and guidance. And finally, to all of the crafters who've shared their advice and experiences with me over the years, thank you for your honesty and openness. This book is better because of you.

Trademarks

All terms mentioned in this book that are known to be or are suspected of being trademarks or service marks have been appropriately capitalized. Alpha Books and Penguin Group (USA) Inc. cannot attest to the accuracy of this information. Use of a term in this book should not be regarded as affecting the validity of any trademark or service mark.

Part 1

First Things First

Even if you never plan on turning craft sales into a serious business, it's important to get started on the right foot. This first part of this book shows you how. You'll start by deciding whether you're really ready to start selling. Then we'll take a practical look at how and where you might decide to sell your crafts, who you might sell them to, and how you can connect with other craft sellers for support, advice, and friendship.

Finally, I'll help you prepare for the adventure by setting up your work space and getting ready for some simple bookkeeping. I'll also introduce you to the different types of taxes that you may eventually need to file as a craft seller.

Chapter 1

Are You Really Ready?

In This Chapter

- Making sure your crafts are ready to sell
- Hobby selling versus selling as a business
- Time and money you need to commit to selling
- Setting reasonable expectations
- Choosing the right time

You have a passion for your craft. You've devoted many hours to honing your skills and developing your own style, and you've learned a lot about yourself in the process. Your craft work is your art: it's part of you, and you have the freedom to approach it just about any way you'd like. Are you ready for the changes that selling might bring? To help you decide, let's take an introductory look at what it takes to sell crafts.

Are Your Crafts Ready?

We'll start with the real stars of your show: your crafts. How do you know that anyone will buy them (besides your mom and your BFF)? Just about all crafts can sell—but only if they're ready. That readiness goes beyond pretty packaging and a nice display. It also requires your crafts to be professional-quality, original designs.

Quality First

The quality of your crafts is massively important. People who buy from crafters are looking for high-quality goods; they expect better products than they can find at their local big-box stores. If your crafts fall apart, then anyone who buys from you won't buy from you again. And if they look sloppy, cheap, or unfinished, you probably won't make any sales at all.

> **Bits and Pieces**
>
> Mastering your craft has advantages beyond ensuring that your work is of good quality. It also enables you to craft faster and more efficiently, which reduces your time commitment—and, as we'll see later, may also help you set better prices.

How can you tell whether your crafts make the grade? First, be honest with yourself. If you started crafting only a few months ago, you probably have a lot to learn. Give yourself a chance to become really good at what you do. Next, think about your crafting process. Are there any techniques that throw you for a loop? If so, spend some more time practicing.

Also do some research. Visit shops, galleries, and websites that feature handmade goods similar to yours. Examine those crafts closely. Take note of the materials used, how they were put together, and the overall look and feel of each piece. (While you're at it, keep an eye on prices, too—they'll help you price your own crafts later.) If your components or techniques seem substandard in any way, take time to fix them before you start selling.

A final note about quality: high quality is not the same as perfect. People expect handcrafted items to have minor variations in shape, texture, and overall appearance. They should look and feel unique and handmade—not made by a machine. Resist the temptation to spend more time than necessary striving for perfection. Not only will you waste time, but you also might even drive off potential customers.

Staying Original

In addition to being good quality, the crafts you sell need to be your own original designs. You should avoid selling anything that's based on a pattern or project in a book or magazine or that you copied from another crafter (unless you have permission). Otherwise, you risk violating someone's copyright. In most countries, the original creator of artwork has the exclusive right to copy or reproduce it—or allow anyone else to—for many years.

You also need to avoid infringing on anyone's trademark rights. A trademark is something that identifies a product or service with a particular individual or business. It can be a business name, a logo, a symbol, or even a cartoon character.

Copyright and trademark issues can result in lawsuits, and copying in general is considered unethical in the crafting community. Use common sense to prevent problems. Don't copy someone else's work outright or knowingly make a design that is very similar to anyone else's unless that person gives you the go ahead. Don't use obvious trademarks, such as logos, in your crafts without permission. And if you use found objects or make collages, read up on copyright and trademark law for artists (some resources are provided in the Supplemental Appendix at www.craftychannels. com/resources)—or if possible, speak with an attorney before you start selling.

Bits and Pieces

Sometimes permission to reproduce craft work is limited to noncommercial use only, meaning that you can make a copy for yourself but can't offer it for sale. This is usually the case with step-by-step craft projects and premade patterns.

The Seller You'd Like to Be

Why do you want to start selling your crafts? You'd probably like to make some extra money while doing what you already enjoy. You might even dream of one day supporting yourself by selling crafts professionally. But no matter how far you'd like to go, there are advantages to starting out small.

The Casual Seller

You can start small by becoming what we'll call a casual seller, where you craft and sell during your free time. Your primary goal is to have fun, make a little extra money, and share your creations with the world. Although you need to do some basic bookkeeping and may need to secure some licenses and permits, you're really more of a hobbyist than a businessperson. You can remain a casual seller forever, or in time you might choose to step up to the next level.

The More Active Seller

We'll refer to that next level as more active selling, where you set real business goals. Your bottom line—or minimum goal—is to cover your costs. Beyond that, you also try to make some degree of profit, which is money left over after your expenses are paid.

To be successful as a more active seller, you need to expose your work to as many people as possible and stay efficient by purchasing supplies in bulk. Because you're typically viewed as a small business, you must carefully keep books, pay business taxes, and stay up-to-date on any business laws that might apply to you. (We'll talk about these and other potential business requirements in later chapters.)

Most crafters never venture beyond this level, but a few brave souls go even farther. I like to think of them as high-commitment sellers who craft and sell full time. In this book, we won't get into the details of running a high-commitment crafting business, but occasionally we'll peek into the special techniques that high-commitment sellers use to succeed.

Devoting Time to Selling

The more serious you become, the greater commitment you'll need to make. A big part of that commitment is the extra time that selling consumes—time beyond that which you already spend crafting for fun. Can you spare it? As you read through the following list of typical craft-selling tasks, think about how you might fit them into your current schedule without throwing your life off balance.

Managing Your Inventory

You already have a collection of supplies that constitute the raw materials, or ingredients, for your crafts. You may even have some projects that are works in progress; you've started them, but they aren't quite finished. As a seller, you have a third category of things to organize and keep track of: the finished goods that you offer for sale. All three categories make up your inventory.

Each part of your inventory requires some care and feeding. With raw materials, you need to spend time purchasing them, organizing them, and tracking their costs. As you use raw materials, you need to keep a record of which become parts of finished goods and in what amounts. Works in progress must be kept clean and organized until they're finished. Finally, you need to safely store, organize, and track your finished goods. We'll start talking about the nuts and bolts of managing inventory in Chapter 4.

Preparing Finished Goods for Sale

Once you have some finished goods, you must prepare them for sale. Probably the most important part of that process is pricing, which we'll cover in Chapter 5. For now, just be aware that successful pricing—setting prices that are fair to you and your customers—requires running some calculations, researching the market, and monitoring your success so that you can make adjustments over time.

Other aspects of preparing your inventory depend on where and how you sell your crafts. For instance, if you sell on the Internet, you need to photograph your finished goods, describe them in writing, and upload the photos and text to a website (see Chapter 9). If you sell in person at shows, you need to pack, transport, unpack, and display your pieces for sale (see Chapters 11 and 17).

Depending on the types of crafts you make, you may also need to spend time maintaining your finished goods. For instance, as a jewelry crafter, I routinely polish items in my inventory that are prone to tarnishing. They must be clean and look their best before I can photograph them, show them, or package them for a customer.

Sale and Postsale Tasks

The very act of offering your work for sale also eats up some time. When you sell online, you monitor and update your sales listings, communicate with customers, process payments, and pack and ship orders. At shows and events, you spend long hours taking care of your display, manning your table or booth, answering questions, and (fingers crossed) handling sales transactions.

After you make a sale, your work isn't always over. Sometimes past customers contact you with questions about their orders or with special requests such as exchanges or size alterations. And even when past customers don't contact you, you'll probably want to keep in touch with them to encourage future sales. Be prepared for this kind of ongoing commitment once you start selling.

Promoting Your Wares

There are probably lots of people in the world who would like to buy your crafts. Unfortunately, it can be difficult to find them and introduce them to your work. In order to secure customers, you'll need to promote your crafts by communicating with people.

As a casual seller, promotion can be as simple as telling your friends and family about your newest designs. More active sellers typically go farther by sending newsletters and announcements of upcoming sales or shows, networking with other crafters, or donating their work to be featured in giveaways, at charity auctions, or in product-review articles. Many also participate in advertising campaigns that take time to manage. We'll dive into these aspects of promotion in Chapters 8 and 16.

Bits and Pieces

How many people do you know right now who might purchase your crafts? If that number is pretty low, plan to devote some extra time to finding customers.

Office Work

Even as a casual seller, you should stay up-to-date with some basic business office work, such as filing receipts and doing simple bookkeeping. It will protect you from potential tax trouble and help you feel more confident overall. More important, you'll be organized and ready if your business starts to really take off. You'll see what I mean in Chapter 12.

Speaking of money, have you thought about how much you'll need to invest in selling your crafts?

Spending to Sell

You've probably heard it hundreds of times: it takes money to make money. While this statement is generally true, you don't have to break the bank to begin selling crafts. If you start small and make savvy decisions, you'll be in a good position to keep things affordable.

Sadly, affordable doesn't mean free. The following are some examples of how most craft sellers spend money on selling. We'll cover them in more detail later. For now, try to imagine how these types of recurring expenses might affect you.

- ◆ **Sales venue fees.** A sales venue is a place, such as a website or craft show, where you can sell your crafts. Most sales venues charge fees. Some charge flat fees, and others take a percentage of your sales.

- ◆ **Transportation and shipping costs.** Whenever you need to transport inventory, whether to offer it for sale somewhere or ship it to a customer, you have costs related to that transportation. These range from purchasing gasoline for your car to software for managing shipments.

- ◆ **Purchasing supplies in bulk.** Buying supplies in large, or bulk, quantities at a discount can reduce your costs and help you make a profit. However, it also requires you to spend more money up front.

- **Payment processing fees.** Payment processors are companies that accept online forms of payment, such as credit cards, on your behalf. Their fees are typically a percentage of your sales, but some also charge recurring flat fees.

- **Costs of promoting your crafts.** Although some sellers promote their work solely by word of mouth, most find it necessary to sign up for special services such as e-mail lists or joint advertising campaigns with other crafters. Many also purchase customized business cards, post cards, and fliers.

- **General business costs.** Taxes and permit or license fees are typical general business costs. Whether you need to file business tax returns or apply for permits and licenses usually depends on how much income you receive from selling your crafts.

What would happen if you didn't make enough sales to cover all these expenses? What if you made no sales at all? Craft sales ebb and flow, and very few beginning craft sellers make as much income as they'd like. If you feel that you can't or shouldn't risk losing any money but still want to sell, it's especially important that you limit yourself to selling very casually until your circumstances change.

 Bits and Pieces

You may hear that you can save money by writing off expenses on your tax returns. Generally, however, that's true in the United States only if you operate a real business—rather than merely sell as a hobby. And even if you run a business, the tax laws place important restrictions on which expenses you can write off and when. We'll look at taxes and write-offs more closely in Chapter 13.

Setting Reasonable Expectations

Finally, what are your personal expectations for success as a craft seller? If you devote a lot of time, energy, and emotional effort to crafting and selling, will you be crushed if your crafts take a long time to sell, sell for less than you'd hoped, or don't sell at all? What if you need to change the way you make your crafts in order to increase sales? Can you maintain that flexibility?

Many budding sellers set overly optimistic goals and then suffer disappointment when they don't achieve them. Understand that it may take a while to find the right venue, develop a customer base, and fine-tune your crafts for selling. Setting realistic expectations early will help you keep enjoying your craft, rather than seeing it as a source of stress or pressure.

Deciding to Sell

Now that you have an idea of what it takes to sell crafts, are you up for it? If you're on the fence, take a little more time to think. Read Chapter 2 and learn about finding your place in the world of craft selling. Visit a craft show and strike up a conversation with a vendor. Hop on the Internet and find other crafters with whom you can share your concerns.

If you decide that now isn't the right time, plan on reevaluating your situation in the future. There's no rush. Your circumstances, your crafts, and possibly even your expectations will evolve. When selling fits into your life without overriding the fun you have crafting, that's the time to go for it.

The Least You Need to Know

- Make sure your crafts are good-quality, original designs.

- Even if you plan to sell very casually, don't get started until you feel comfortable with the time and financial commitments that selling may require.

- Set reasonable expectations about craft selling, and don't assume that you'll make lots of sales right away.

- Don't rush into selling, and make sure that you're really ready for the changes it brings to your crafting life.

Chapter 2

Exploring the Indie Craft Marketplace

In This Chapter

- ◆ Sales channels versus sales venues
- ◆ Selecting sales channels and sales venues
- ◆ Finding help within the crafting community

You can think of the indie craft marketplace as the entire world of independent craft selling. When you sell independently, you sell entirely for your own benefit; you don't work for anyone else. Independence gives you the freedom—but also the responsibility—to make all the important decisions about selling your crafts.

Comparing Sales Channels

In Chapter 1, I defined sales venues as the "where" of craft selling: the places you can sell. Sales channels are the "how" of selling, or the ways you can sell. They include *direct selling*

Term Tag

Direct selling is selling directly to a customer, rather than to a reseller such as a shop owner.

online, direct selling in person, and selling wholesale to resellers. Through sales channels, you show your work to potential customers, receive money for purchases, and deliver finished goods to people who buy them.

Sales venues are categorized by the sales channels they use, as shown in the following diagram.

The relationship between sales channels and sales venues.

Direct Selling Online

When you sell online, you publish photos and written descriptions of your finished goods on a website. Visitors to the site can make purchases by clicking links and entering payment and shipping information. When you receive confirmation that payment has cleared, you package the customer's order and mail it.

The most popular online sales venues fall into three categories, which we'll examine more closely in later chapters:

♦ Shopping sites (sometimes called online marketplaces), where your crafts appear along with many other items for sale from other vendors.

♦ Auction sites, where potential customers "bid" on items rather than purchase them at set prices.

♦ Standalone websites that you create and control yourself.

The main benefits of selling online are:

- **Flexibility.** You can work entirely from home and set your own hours. You can also change your presentation, prices, and inventory selection whenever you choose.

- **Cost.** You can minimize your costs of selling, especially if you use a shopping site with reasonable fees.

- **Exposure.** You can stay behind the scenes if you're not a people person and don't enjoy pushing sales in person.

And here are some potential downsides:

- **Competition.** There are many online sellers these days, and it's difficult to stand out in the crowd.

- **Time commitment.** Photographing, writing descriptions, and updating websites can be time-consuming.

- **Customer experience.** Potential customers cannot touch, feel, or (if you sell clothing or accessories) try on your goods. Additionally, because you and your customers don't see one another in person, it's more difficult for you to target them and for them to gain trust in you.

Hitting a Snag

Don't assume that listing your crafts for sale online will automatically attract customers. It's not easy to get noticed on the Internet. You need to promote your work in other ways and actively drive traffic to whichever website you use. We'll cover some ways to do this, such as using e-mail lists, social networking sites, and advertising, in Chapters 8, 15, and 16.

Direct Selling in Person

Selling in person, where you meet customers face-to-face, is another form of direct selling. You have two options here: taking your crafts to potential customers, or bringing potential customers to your crafts. Either way, you serve as a sales clerk, processing each sales transaction when it happens.

The three most common sales venues that use these techniques are:

- ◆ Trunk shows, where you display your crafts for sale either alone or with a small group of other sellers

- ◆ Sales parties, where you invite potential customers to your home or studio

- ◆ Craft shows and other organized events, where multiple sellers display their wares side by side

Here are the most important benefits of selling in person:

- ◆ **Flexibility.** You choose the dates and times that you offer your goods for sale, making it easier to budget your time.

- ◆ **Customer experience.** Customers can touch, feel, and inspect your goods in person—and you can monitor their reactions when they do.

And here are this channel's primary downsides:

- ◆ **Exposure.** You need to present an uplifting persona to potential customers, even if you're feeling tired, unwell, or uncomfortable. You can also be exposed to difficult people or situations, and your goods may be at risk of theft by shoplifters.

- ◆ **Time commitment.** In addition to crafting enough finished goods to present for sale, you need to transport them to sales venues and set up your own displays, which can include tables, chairs, lights, and even a tent.

Selling to Resellers

A reseller is someone who buys your crafts at wholesale prices and sells them at retail prices through their own sales venue. Wholesale prices are the discounted prices that you offer resellers in exchange for volume purchases; retail prices are the marked-up prices resellers charge their own customers for the same items. Shops, boutiques, and galleries are typical craft resellers.

Here are some benefits of selling to resellers:

◆ **Faster payment.** You receive payment sooner than if you sold the same goods individually.

◆ **Convenience.** You can market all your wares to one reseller, rather than devoting time to individual retail customers. Additionally, the reseller—rather than you—has the responsibility of selling your goods before they fall out of fashion or lose their usefulness.

◆ **Growth potential.** Wholesale accounts can lead to more wholesale accounts, helping your business grow faster if you decide to become a serious seller.

But selling to resellers can also have these disadvantages:

◆ **Customer experience.** You have limited control over how your crafts are displayed and presented.

◆ **Cost.** You make less money per item than when you sell retail.

◆ **Time commitment.** For some wholesale orders, you may need to produce a large number of finished goods under a deadline.

Bits and Pieces

When you're just starting, you might choose to sell in stores or galleries under consignment, rather than selling wholesale. With consignment, you don't receive any payment until your goods are purchased by retail customers. Consignment opportunities can be easier to secure than wholesale orders, but they're also tricky business. We'll talk more about them in Chapter 18.

Managing Multiple Sales Channels

You're not limited to using just one sales channel. For example, you may decide to list your crafts for sale on a shopping site and also peddle them at trunk shows. You can make more sales with this kind of diversity, but it requires you to stay well organized. You must keep track of the status of all your finished goods so you don't mistakenly offer something for sale in two places or forget which item sold through which venue.

In addition, you may need to use different payment processing methods for different sales channels. For instance, many crafters process payments differently online than they do in person. Multiple channels (and venues) can also affect how you price your crafts, as we'll see in Chapter 5.

Selecting Sales Venues

Once you decide on one or more sales channels, you can start to select venues within them. Look for venues that are convenient and affordable but that also reflect your style and attract the right customers.

Defining Your Style

Are your crafts influenced by a trend such as Hollywood glam, mid-century mod, or nouveau-hippie green? Or do you ignore trends, blurring the line between craftwork and art? It's important to understand and define your style and then find sales venues to match it.

Sales venues have styles of their own, which you can usually recognize through their advertising. A venue that uses clean and simple designs may have a contemporary, hipster feel while one with heavy, ornate designs might have a Victorian Revival theme. These styles are important to pay attention to because they target different types of customers.

Targeting Your Customers

As I pointed out in Chapter 1, not just anyone will buy your crafts. You need to identify that select group of people who will: your target customers. These are the people you *market* to. Once you know them, you can select sales venues they're likely to use.

Exactly who will value, appreciate, and really crave your work? What's their income level? How do they dress? What music do they listen to? What are their hobbies and interests? The style of your crafts should help you answer these ques-

Term Tag

To **market** goods or services means to create, offer, promote, and deliver them to customers.

tions. If you construct pincushions shaped like computer mice, your target customers are probably young-spirited, computer-savvy crafters who sew. If you make hemp jewelry, your target customers likely enjoy the outdoors, are environmentally aware, and eschew celebrity fashion.

Your customers won't all fit into one mold, but they will have some important things in common. You can use those commonalities to reach out to them. We'll explore some ways to do that in Chapter 8.

Thinking about Prices

Your crafts' price range is an important factor when selecting a venue. Even if you haven't priced out any of your crafts, you should have a general idea of their value—or what your target customers will expect to pay for them. For example, if you make higher-end luxury goods, galleries or websites that feature fine art may be a better fit than auction sites that attract bargain hunters.

Looking in the Mirror to Find Your Niche

Thinking about your own style, tastes, and expectations as a shopper can help you select sales venues. After all, if your crafts appeal to you, you're probably a lot like your target customers. Where do you like to shop? Are there venues that you avoid?

Remember that even if your crafts are wonderful quality, unique, reasonably priced, and beautifully presented, they will not sell well in a venue that doesn't suit them. You must find their perfect niche.

Making Connections in the Crafting Community

Independence as a craft seller doesn't mean isolation. There's a thriving crafting community you can access for tips and advice, motivation, and promotional opportunities. Let's explore some ways to find and connect with other craft sellers. For more specific resources, see the Supplemental Appendix at www.craftychannels.com/resources.

Crafters Online

There are lots of websites devoted to bringing crafters together—and many of the crafters you meet online are also sellers. You can ask them questions in forums or live chats or by commenting on their blogs. Look for sites that focus on your particular craft as well as general crafting sites.

Social networking sites such as Facebook and MySpace are also popular with crafters. You use them by setting up a profile page and then adding other people as friends or followers. Many allow you to join craft-specific groups or networks. You can also find social networking sites developed entirely for crafters.

Microblogging services, such as Twitter, are also good for locating fellow crafters. You can search for relevant posts, follow or message other crafters, and reply to their comments.

SOLD | **Selling Secrets**

Don't take anything you read online too seriously. Although the Internet is a great source of information and a convenient way to meet people, it's also rife with bad advice—and the occasional bad apple. Never make an important decision based solely on something posted online. (Incorrect business and tax information is especially common.) If you receive a rude or negative comment in a forum or on a blog, do your best to let it go. It's probably not anything you did wrong; it's just the seamy side of the Internet.

Magazines

Craft magazines often contain articles about selling, including reviews of shopping sites and interviews with successful sellers. Browse the racks at larger book stores or craft supply stores to find them. Just as with websites, you might find specialty magazines for your particular craft in addition to general crafting titles.

Local Clubs and Groups

In many cities, local craft sellers team up to motivate one another, network, and socialize. Some even produce their own newsletters. To find them, run Internet searches using the name of your town and terms such as "crafts" and "handmade." You can also ask at local craft shows or check the club directories in craft magazines. If all else fails, grab some friends and start your own group.

Bits and Pieces

Businesses that sell craft supplies can be valuable sources of information about raw materials, crafting techniques, and even sales strategies. When you find an interesting supplier online or in person—especially one that specializes in your craft medium—inquire whether they have a newsletter or regular catalog. The savviest suppliers offer these by e-mail or regular mail to notify you about sales and new stock and to give you tips and advice to motivate you to keep crafting.

The Least You Need to Know

◆ Sales channels are methods for selling your crafts. You should select a sales channel first, then look for a sales venue that uses it.

◆ Don't waste time on sales channels or venues that aren't right for your crafts.

◆ Your crafts' style, the identity of your target customers, and your price range are all important factors for choosing sales channels and venues.

◆ Other sellers in the crafting community can offer you valuable tips and help you stay motivated. Find them online, through magazines, or in your local community.

Chapter 3

The Bare Necessities of Selling

In This Chapter

- ◆ Designating and arranging your work spaces
- ◆ Establishing ways to communicate
- ◆ Getting started with bookkeeping and filing
- ◆ Understanding taxes

You'll have more fun and less frustration selling crafts if you start out well prepared. In this chapter, I'll walk you through the basics of getting set up and ready to sell. Because most tasks we'll cover are typical business startup activities, you can learn more about them by consulting general business books, magazines, and websites such as the ones listed in the Supplemental Appendix at www.craftychannels.com/resources.

Staking Out Your Space

You should designate a work space in your home or studio for each phase of the selling process: designing and creating, packaging and shipping, and office work. If possible, make them separate spaces that are located conveniently near one another. They don't need to be huge, but they should be smartly laid out and well-organized. Each space should be stocked with essential supplies—some of which you can wait to purchase until after you start making sales.

A Place to Create

You already have a work space for crafting. It might be stationary, such as a table or desk, or you might keep things portable with a box or bag of necessities that you carry with you. How is it working? Do you stay organized and comfortable while you work? Do you have adequate lighting? If not, now is a good time to make improvements.

Your crafting work space should include places to store tools, supplies, and raw materials in a neat and orderly way. Use stick-on labels to identify items or categories of items in your raw materials. If you need help organizing particular items, ask around in the crafting community. You can save time and money by learning from the experience of other people who specialize in your craft medium.

Your Personal Sales Desk

You also need a desk or table where you can do office work, such as simple bookkeeping, writing product descriptions, and processing orders. This is where you should set up your computer and phone. Keep it free from the clutter of craft-making materials and stocked with typical home office supplies, including pens, blank notepaper, and a calculator. Place a file cabinet or file box nearby for storing important paperwork. Try to place your computer's printer within close reach.

To conserve space, you can transform a closet or armoire into an office area. Browse through home design and crafting magazines for ideas; some even publish issues devoted entirely to small home offices or craft spaces. See the Supplemental Appendix at www.craftychannels.com/resources for some recommendations.

Crafty Computing

Before we move on to the next work space, let's talk about your computer. I strongly recommend that you use one, even if you never sell online. You can save time and stay better organized by using a basic word-processing program or spreadsheet to track inventory and sales, calculate prices, and track your overall progress. If you have an Internet connection, you can shop for supplies, research the marketplace, print postage, and communicate with customers and other crafters with ease.

Make sure your Internet connection is fast enough to avoid frustrating slowdowns when uploading and downloading digital files. Install photo-editing software on your computer, and use a quality monitor that depicts digital photos as accurately as possible.

If you don't have a computer or don't like computing, plan on using lots of notebooks and pens or pencils. Designate shelf space for keeping notebooks accessible and organized, and decide how best to label them. You might write on their covers with a permanent marker or use a label-making machine from an office supply store to generate stickers.

Setting Up a Shipping Area

If you sell online, you need a shipping area. At a minimum, it should provide a clean, flat surface for packaging orders and enough space for essential shipping supplies. Those supplies might include:

- Ballpoint pens and permanent markers
- Scissors
- Household adhesive tape and packaging tape
- Paper sorting trays
- Cushioning packaging material (such as bubble wrap)
- Envelopes in various sizes and thicknesses
- Cardboard shipping boxes
- Gift boxes and gift bags
- Decorative tissue paper and ribbon

- A postage scale
- Blank shipping labels

Whether you use envelopes or boxes depends on the size, weight, and sturdiness of your crafts. Small, lightweight, and nonbreakable items can ship in extra-strong envelopes called mailers. Heavy or fragile goods require cardboard boxes with lots of cushioning material.

You can save money—and help the environment—by reusing cardboard boxes and using crumpled newspaper as cushioning material. But only do this if your target customers are people who admire such efforts. If you promote your crafts as high-end luxury items, your customers will probably expect more professional-looking packaging.

Bits and Pieces

The U.S. Postal Service (USPS), United Parcel Service (UPS), FedEx, and other shippers provide specially marked envelopes, boxes, and labels for free. However, you can use them only for certain services, such as priority mail or express delivery.

Gift boxes, gift bags, colored tissue paper, and ribbon are packaging materials that personalize your crafts and entice customers to buy again. You should protect them with standard mailers or boxes used for shipping.

Some supplies, such as postage scales and blank shipping labels, are optional. Whether you need them depends on how you buy postage. For example, if you print postage on your computer, you don't need write-on labels, but you do need labels or paper (for taping onto packages) for your printer. If you weigh packages at the post office, you might not need your own scale (although it's still useful for estimating shipping costs).

You can find basic shipping supplies at most office supply stores. You'll save money in the long run by buying in bulk whenever possible, especially with tape, envelopes, boxes, and cushioning material.

Getting Ready to Communicate

Communicating is a big part of selling. This section covers your options for keeping in touch with customers and other important people remotely (when you can't visit them in person). You may decide to use all of these techniques or just one or two. Select what works best for you.

Connecting Online

There are many ways to communicate with people online. E-mail is a staple; it's convenient and available to just about anyone with an Internet connection. To appear more professional and protect your privacy, set up a separate e-mail account for craft selling. You can print its address on business cards and other marketing materials and use it to contact customers and suppliers directly.

If you decide to use an assumed name as a seller instead of your actual name (see Chapter 6), try to include it in your e-mail address. You can start with a free e-mail service, such as Gmail or Yahoo! Mail, and use your business name as your account name. Later, you may decide to purchase your own domain name to use for e-mail (we'll cover that process in Chapter 16).

Bits and Pieces

Most online shopping sites offer ways for sellers and buyers to exchange private messages without using e-mail. For instance, on Etsy (www.etsy.com), you can send and receive messages called conversations, or "convos." This doesn't keep you from needing an e-mail address, but it can be a more reliable and convenient way to reach customers. We'll revisit this topic in Chapter 9.

Working the Phone

Even if the Internet is your primary mode of communication, there will be times when you need to pick up the phone and talk to someone. It might be a customer with a question or concern about an order or a supplier having trouble processing your credit card. A phone also comes in handy for staying in touch with resellers who are interested in your work.

If you sell very casually, your regular home phone or personal cell phone is probably all you need. But if you become more active, you should set up a separate phone line or service for business use. It will give you a number to print on business cards without jeopardizing your privacy and will make it easier to track phone-related expenses because you'll have a separate bill.

The old-school way of starting a new phone line (also called a landline) is to hire the phone company to install one in your home. But today, you have more convenient—and sometimes more affordable—options as well, such as purchasing a second cell phone or signing up with an online phone service.

You can find online phone service providers by searching the Internet. For some services, you need a head set that plugs into your computer. With others, you are given a device that connects a regular phone to your computer. For these services to work, your computer typically must be switched on. More expensive services offer a phone and modem that work over the Internet independent of your computer.

Before you select a phone service, read through its policies (called terms of service, or TOS) and talk with a customer service representative if you have questions. Find out whether there are minutes caps, fees for long distance, or other extra charges that you may want to minimize or avoid.

Traditional Mail

You can use traditional mail to receive mail-order supplies and notices, catalogs, magazines, and newsletters related to crafts and selling. You might also use it to ship orders or send promotional materials to customers.

In any case, you usually need to disclose your address to other people— either as a delivery address or as a return address. To keep your home address private, you can rent an offsite mail box. There are two places to find them: the local post office or a private mail box provider. Both have advantages and disadvantages.

Post office boxes are economical and conveniently located, especially if you visit the post office often. However, the address you receive always contains the abbreviation "P.O." followed by your box number. This means you cannot use it as a "street address," which is sometimes required by sales venues and agencies that issue permits and licenses. Post office boxes also cannot accept deliveries from private shippers, such as UPS or FedEx.

Private mail boxes, such as the ones available from Mail Boxes Etc. or The UPS Store, are usually pricier than post office boxes. However, their addresses qualify as street addresses because they do not contain "P.O." These boxes can also receive deliveries from private shipping companies. Packages that are too large to fit in your box are usually held behind the counter until you pick them up.

Setting Up Books and Files

Bookkeeping is the process of recording revenue (money coming in) and expenses (money going out). You "keep books" to monitor your progress and comply with tax, licensing, and permitting laws. Your "books" are actually ongoing logs, or journals. They can be in the form of computer spreadsheets, special bookkeeping software, or notebooks.

Files refer to the physical files and folders that you store in or near your office work space. You use them to keep paper copies of receipts that back up the information in your bookkeeping journals. You can also use them for storing important paperwork such as tax documents, permits, licenses, and wholesale and consignment contracts. You should plan on keeping the papers in your files for many years after their original dates. Transfer some to storage boxes if your file cabinet ever becomes full.

Bookkeeping vs. Accounting

Bookkeeping is not the same as accounting. Accounting is the process of categorizing, summarizing, and reporting the information in your bookkeeping journals. You use accounting to report revenue and expenses on your tax returns. (We'll talk more about taxes later.) Optionally, you can purchase small business bookkeeping and accounting software that automatically generates accounting reports.

Tracking Revenue and Expenses

You should set up your books before you spend much money or begin making sales. To keep it simple, you can start by creating two separate journals: one for expenses and one for revenue. (If you purchase book-keeping software, these may be created for you—but it's still important to understand how they work.)

Let's start with an expense journal. For each expense related to selling, you need to record the date, description, who you paid (called the vendor), and the amount. You might set up your expense journal like this one, which includes its first few entries:

Sample Beginning Expense Journal

Date	Vendor	Description	Amount Paid
01/12	Davis Bead Co.	Seed beads	$35.72
01/31	Max's Shipping Supplies	Bubble wrap	$8.99
02/03	Crafts on the Net	Shopping site fee	$15.00

Now set up a similar journal for revenue. For each sale, you need to record the date, product description, sales price, and any separate sales tax or shipping fees that you charge. Here's an example of a revenue journal with its first few entries:

Sample Beginning Revenue Journal

Date	Item	Price	Shipping	Total Received
01/07	Wrapped hoop earrings	$24.00	$2.50	$26.50
01/18	Beaded bookmark	$8.00	$2.50	$10.50
02/12	Daisy chain lanyard	$12.00	$2.50	$14.50

You don't need to update your journals at the very moment an expense or sale takes place. It's usually easier to use receipts to make updates at logical, regular intervals, such as once per week or per month and immediately following busy events such as craft shows. Also make a habit of totaling your journal entries at least monthly so you can compare your expenses and revenue. This gives you a snapshot of how you did for the month and helps with long-term budgeting.

Filing Receipts

To save and organize receipts, set up at least two file folders: one for receipts that you prepare for customers and another for receipts, invoices, or statements that you receive from vendors. Inside each folder, place a file labeled "Unentered" (we'll return to these shortly). Then designate a file for each venue and vendor that you use. You can organize them as follows:

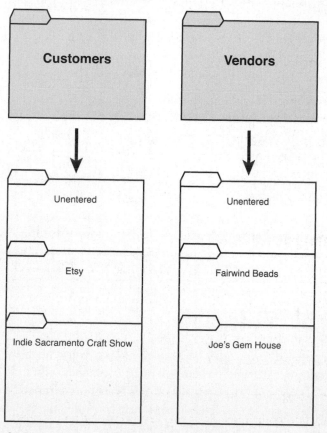

Setting up folders and files for paper receipts.

Plan to give sales receipts to all your customers. At a minimum, each receipt should contain the information you record in your revenue journal, plus your name and contact information. You can make receipts by hand or on your computer, but the best way to generate copies when you sell in person is to use duplicate receipts that you fill in by hand. These are sold in pads and notebooks at office supply stores. If you prefer something more stylish, you can always give your customers two receipts: one that you creatively designed and one from a duplicate receipt pad. After you make a sale, place a copy of the sales receipt in the Unentered file in your Customers folder.

When you sell online, the website you use may automatically generate receipts or "order summaries" for you and your customers. In that case, you can simply print copies of those for your files.

Whenever you purchase craft or office supplies, place a copy of the vendor's receipt or invoice in the Unentered file in your Vendors folder. Make sure that each vendor receipt is labeled clearly with its date, the vendor's name, a list of the items you purchased, the amount you paid for each item, the total paid, and the payment method.

Keep in mind that some vendors do not itemize their receipts. (This is common at large sales events, such as bead shows.) In those circumstances, you need to keep notes describing the quantity and price of each item that you purchase. Staple those notes to the vendor receipts before filing them.

To update your bookkeeping records, enter all the sales and vendor receipts from your Unentered files. Put a check mark or other symbol on each receipt to confirm that you've entered it, then move it to the appropriate venue or vendor name file. This makes it easy to determine where you left off the next time you make updates.

Staying Out of Tax Trouble

Even if you sell very casually, you may be required to pay some taxes on your craft-selling income. And even when you don't owe taxes, you may still be required to file certain tax returns. For this reason, it's important to research the laws where you live and monitor your tax status. Keep in mind that if you begin to make more sales over time, you may become subject to taxes that did not apply to you before.

We'll talk more about how to obtain permits and licenses and file tax returns in Chapter 13. For now, take a few minutes to learn which types of taxes might apply to you and why.

Income Taxes

As a general rule, you must pay federal and state personal income taxes if your total income from all sources exceeds a certain amount. You must report craft sales as part of that income. If you make enough sales over time, you might be allowed to reduce the taxes you owe by deducting business expenses. Keep saving your expense receipts, and we'll revisit this later.

State and Local Business Taxes

Business taxes are often collected by state or local agencies through business licenses, based on the revenue businesses report when they renew their licenses. In some places, a business license is required if you do any routine selling—whether or not you make a profit. To request a business license, you need to fill out an application—and you'll likely be charged a small application fee. Be sure to check with your city, county, or state to learn its requirements and ask about possible exceptions for small, home-based businesses.

Sales Tax

In many U.S. states, sales tax is collected by a state tax agency. Generally, you must file sales tax returns with that agency if it requires you to have a seller's permit (sometimes called a resale permit). Contact your state tax agency to find out whether you need one, which may depend on how many sales you make and how much revenue you generate from them.

To request a seller's permit, you simply fill out and submit an application, which may or may not include a small fee. Your seller's permit should arrive in the mail along with instructions for reporting and paying sales tax. Remember that although you can charge your customers for sales tax, it's your responsibility to file a return and remit that tax to the state.

Selling Secrets _____

Be on the lookout for any permits that you may need apart from a business license and seller's permit. For instance, many local governments require that you apply for a home-based business permit if you work from home, and you may be subject to special state or federal safety regulations if your products are edible or potentially hazardous. You can usually find out about these by asking around in the crafting community.

The Least You Need to Know

◆ Maintain neat, organized work spaces for crafting, doing office work, and (if you sell online) preparing orders for shipment.

◆ Establish ways to communicate as a seller using the Internet, a phone, and mail.

◆ Before you start selling, set up some simple bookkeeping records and receipt files.

◆ The taxes most likely to apply to craft sellers are income taxes, business license taxes, and sales tax. Find out which might apply to you and monitor your tax status over time.

Part 2

Getting Started as a Casual Seller

Now it's time to really get to work. In this part, you'll assemble an inventory, price your wares, define your crafts' style, and draw up some initial business policies and practices.

By the end of Chapter 7, you should know what to sell first—and, even more importantly, how to go about processing your first sales transactions. We'll then take an introductory look at what you can do to start promoting your crafts, from simply chatting with friends to writing newsletters and blog posts.

Chapter 4

Creating and Managing Inventory

In This Chapter

- ◆ How to keep track of important information about raw materials
- ◆ The types of designs you can sell
- ◆ Premade goods versus made-to-order goods
- ◆ How to establish and organize your first finished goods inventory

Once you have some crafts ready to sell, you could simply place them in a sales venue and see what happens. This is how many sellers get started—but most later regret not taking more time to prepare. They have trouble with pricing, budgeting, tracking their progress, and (when sales start to take off) accurately deducting expenses on their tax returns.

The purpose of this chapter is to help you avoid those problems by properly managing your inventory, as small as it may be, from the very beginning. First, we'll whip your raw materials into shape. Then we'll prepare and organize your initial finished goods. By the end of the chapter, you'll be in an excellent position to move forward and sell with confidence.

Keeping Track of Raw Materials

Raw materials are the building blocks of your crafts. If you sew, they include things such as fabric and thread. If you make pottery, they include clay and glaze. Raw materials can be unique items, where no two pieces are alike, or *stock* items.

Term Tag

Stock materials are nonunique items that are ordinarily available for repurchase whenever your supply runs low. For example, if you're a ceramic artist, your favorite pottery clay is probably a stock material.

You need to track your raw materials in order to determine the cost of each of your finished goods. Those costs are important for pricing, and at some point you may also need them for tax purposes.

Setting Up Raw Materials Inventory Records

You can track raw materials by keeping raw materials inventory sheets. Use them to record which raw materials you have on hand, their quantities, the suppliers you purchased them from, and how much you paid for them.

The following is an example of how you can set up each sheet. Alternatively, you can use an affordable, premade tracking spreadsheet that you download to your computer.

Sample Blank Raw Materials Inventory Sheet

Item: _____ Category: _____ Unit Type: _____

Date	Transaction	Supplier	Finished Goods	Number of Units	Amount Paid	Cost Per Unit

Sample raw materials inventory sheet.

Here's what each heading on the sheet means:

Item is the name or a brief description of the material.

Category is helpful if your raw materials fall into logical groupings.

Unit type refers to the quantity or measurement that you track a material in, such as pieces, inches, or yards.

Date is the date that you purchased or used the material.

Transaction is the type of transaction that increases or decreases your raw materials on hand. The most common transactions are "Purchases" and "Use" in finished goods.

Supplier is who sold you the raw material.

Finished goods refer to items you craft using raw materials.

Number of units is the quantity of raw materials you have on hand.

Amount paid is the purchase price of the raw material.

Cost per unit is how much you paid per unit of the material.

You should create a sheet for each raw material you plan to use in finished goods. For the first entry, enter "Starting" as the Transaction and leave the Amount Paid blank. Under Number of Units, write how many units of the material you have. I've provided a sample sheet with some entries filled in later in the chapter. Before we look at it, let's cover some more information that can help you get started.

 Bits and Pieces

> If you can't remember what something is, where it came from, or how much it cost, make an informed guess. Search for similar items on the Internet or look through product catalogs for clues. Use asterisks or other symbols on your raw materials sheets to denote entries that are guesses.

Counting Raw Materials

When you track raw materials, you should use units that are convenient based on how you make your crafts. For example, if you knit shawls that consume several skeins of yarn each, your units might be skeins or half skeins.

Some raw materials are more difficult to quantify because of their form or size. Such materials are usually sold by weight or volume rather than by piece or length. One way to track them is by using a fraction of the unit they're sold in and then estimating how much you use when you craft. I often take this approach with tiny seed beads that I purchase by the gram. If I buy a 5-gram tube and typically use at least $\frac{1}{5}$ of a tube per project, I can use $\frac{1}{5}$ of 5 grams (or $\frac{5}{5}$) to define a unit as 1 gram.

When you have a hard-to-count supply that is very inexpensive in the amount you use it in, such as glue, you can treat it as an incidental ingredient instead of a raw material. These are categorized as general selling expenses that go into your overhead (see Chapter 5).

Costing Raw Materials

To calculate cost per unit, you divide the total amount paid by the number of units that you purchased. When you buy in units that are larger than the units you track, however, you first need to perform a conversion. As a jewelry crafter, I do this with bead-stringing cable. A typical spool contains 100 feet of cable, but I track cable by the inch. Because there are 1,200 inches in 100 feet, I divide the cost of the spool by 1,200. If I paid $35 for a spool, my cost per inch is then $^{28}/_{1,200}$, or about 3¢.

Updating Raw Materials Inventory Records

Update your inventory records whenever you purchase or use raw materials. Following is the sample sheet from earlier with its starting information filled in and several updates entered.

For each new transaction, enter a new line of information derived from your receipt for a purchase or your product information sheet (which we'll get to later in this chapter) for a use. Purchases increase your number of units, and uses decrease them. At any point on a sheet, you can use a blank line to total the number of units on hand and the amount paid to date. You can also calculate your average cost per unit, as shown on the sample sheet, when the prices of materials fluctuate.

Updated Sample Raw Materials Inventory Sheet

Item: <u>6mm round onyx beads</u> **Category:** <u>Stone Beads</u>   **Unit Type:** Bead

Date	Transaction	Supplier	Finished Goods	Number of Units	Amount Paid	Cost Per Unit
01/01/10	Starting	Fairwind Beads*	—	60	—	$0.08*
01/14/10	Purchase	Joe's Gem House	—	45	$4.05	$0.09
02/05/10	Use	—	Mallorca Necklace	-12	—	—
02/17/10	Use	—	Mallorca Bracelet	-6	—	—
03/07/10	Purchase	Joe's Gem House	—	40	$2.80	$0.07
Totals:				127	$6.85	
Average Cost Per Unit:						$0.08

* = estimate

Updated sample raw materials inventory sheet.

Understanding Finished Goods

You can't start selling until you have something to sell. Before you decide what to offer first, let's examine the types of designs you can sell and the differences between premade and made-to-order goods.

Design Options

Your finished goods inventory can contain any combination of the following types of designs:

♦ **One-of-a-kind designs,** which are unique and never reproduced

♦ **Limited edition designs,** which you reproduce a limited number of times

♦ **Stock (or unlimited) designs,** which you can reproduce indefinitely

The style of your crafts and your target customers' expectations should guide you in deciding which to offer. If your crafts are highly artistic and your customers are collectors, your inventory should include at least some one-of-a-kind designs. But if your customers are twenty-somethings with a strong sense of style and limited spending money, stock designs might be a better bet. As we'll see in the next chapter, you can usually price stock items lower than one-of-a-kind items.

Limited edition designs are a compromise between those two. They have more value than stock designs and take less time to produce than one-of-a-kind pieces. They're also a good option when you have a limited supply of unique raw materials.

> **SOLD** **Selling Secrets**
>
> One-of-a-kind designs are often labeled or described with the acronym "OOAK." When you sell online, you can use OOAK in your listing titles or key words to help potential customers find your one-of-a-kind items in searches.

Custom orders, where you make something for a customer by request based on that customer's unique requirements, are one-of-a-kind designs. Custom orders take more time to fulfill because you need to work closely with your customer to create a design that meets his or her needs and stays within the requested price range while also adhering to your quality standards.

Premade or Made to Order?

Finished goods that you craft and keep on hand until they sell are called premade. Once you start making sales, you might decide to eliminate or reduce the size of your premade inventory by selling crafts made to order. You don't actually craft made-to-order goods until someone purchases them. Initially, you present samples or photographs for potential customers to examine. When an item is purchased, you agree to complete a copy for the customer within a set period of time, called turnaround time.

Selling made-to-order designs reduces the inventory storage space you need, and it allows you to offer custom sizes for handmade clothing and accessories. It also reduces the chance that you'll get stuck with items that never sell.

On the other hand, some customers prefer premade goods for instant gratification or for purchasing gifts under a deadline. Made-to-order goods typically sell better online than in person, because online customers are more open to waiting for their orders to arrive. But wherever you sell them, be sure to inform potential customers that they are made to order, and always provide an estimated turnaround time.

How Much to Offer First

Your initial finished goods inventory should be large enough to demonstrate your style and legitimacy as a seller but small enough to easily manage. Try to start with at least 5 to 15 designs, even if they're all similar. You don't need to offer something for everyone—just something for your target customers.

Crafting and Tracking Finished Goods

In order to accurately price your wares, you need to track your design time, your crafting ("assembly") time, and the raw materials you use. To track these properly, you can use records called product information sheets.

Setting Up Product Information Sheets

The figure on the next page shows a sample product information sheet for a hypothetical beaded necklace. You can design your sheets the same way or customize them to better suit your needs.

The entries for Cost Per Unit on this sheet are the Average Cost Per Unit figures from your raw materials inventory sheets. Notice that when you record Quantity Used on a product information sheet, you also need to subtract that number from Number of Units on the corresponding raw materials inventory sheet (see the 6mm round onyx beads as an example). If you have trouble remembering how many units of something you used, make an estimate. Remember to include any waste materials, such as trimmed-off and discarded segments of wire, yarn, or fabric, in your totals.

For any item you've already completed without a product inventory sheet, go back and make one now.

Sample Product Information Sheet

Item: Mallorca Necklace   **Category:** Necklaces

Design Time: 1 hour   **Assembly Time:** 30 minutes   **Date Completed:** 02/05/10

Type of Design: Limited Edition (maximum 30 copies)

Raw Material Component	Quantity Used	Cost Per Unit	Total Cost
6mm round onyx beads	12 beads	$0.08	$0.96
Sterling silver star pendant	1 piece	$7.95	$7.95
Silver leaf drops	6 pieces	$0.89	$5.34
20-gauge silver-plated wire	6 inches	$0.65	$3.90
Bead-stringing cable	25 inches	$0.03	$0.75
2mm silver crimp tubes	2 pieces	$0.45	$0.90
Silver toggle clasp set	1 piece	$4.99	$4.99
Final Total:			**$24.79**

Sample product information sheet.

Updating Product Information Sheets

Over time, you may find it helpful to add more information to your product information sheets. For example, if you make more than one copy of a design, you can record that number. You can also add pricing information.

Keeping a Finished Goods Inventory List

Finally, as you complete each finished good, you should add it to another type of record: your finished goods inventory list. Its main purpose is to track which and how many finished goods you have on hand at a given time. You can also use it to track sales venues, prices, and sales, as shown in the following example. Notice that because I haven't decided on a venue or price for the Mallorca necklace, I left those fields blank.

Sample Finished Goods Inventory List

Category: Necklaces

Item	Date Completed	Sales Venue	Retail Price	Date Sold
Santander Necklace	01/01/10	Etsy	$55.00	1/31/10
39th Avenue Choker	01/16/10	Consignment— Nancy's Boutique	$38.00	
Mallorca Necklace	02/05/10		$	

Sample finished goods inventory list.

Hitting a Snag

Do your best to avoid getting behind with updating your inventory sheets and lists. They're much easier to manage if you work on them incrementally, rather than procrastinating and attempting to update many entries at once.

The Least You Need to Know

- ♦ Even if you have a small inventory, you should carefully track your raw materials and finished goods.

- ♦ Track raw materials by recording how many you have, where you purchased them, and how much they cost.

- ♦ Track finished goods by recording the time it takes to design and craft them and the cost of raw materials used to make them.

- ♦ Keep a running list of your finished goods.

Chapter 5

Pricing It Out

In This Chapter

◆ Estimating prices by compiling costs and using markups

◆ Refining price estimates

◆ Changing prices and reducing costs over time

◆ Alternatives to lowering prices and reducing costs

◆ Setting prices for multiple sales channels or venues

As a general business rule, you should price your goods high enough to cover your costs and to make some profit without going beyond what most of your target customers are willing to pay. You can estimate target prices by running some calculations and researching the market. But how much work you really put into pricing depends on your selling goals. If you're not too concerned about making a profit, you can estimate your prices more loosely.

This chapter offers a complete approach to setting prices that follow the general business rule. If you'd like to begin on a more casual level, you can skim over the first few pages of this chapter and use the section "Narrowing Down Price Ranges" to make rough price estimates based on the market. If you get more serious later, be sure to revisit the entire chapter to set your prices more accurately.

Pricing Basics

There are lots of pricing techniques, but most follow a common methodology: use formulas to make initial price estimates, then refine those estimates based on practical factors and savvy guesses. Over time, you can use your bookkeeping records to track how well your goods sell at which prices and adjust prices accordingly.

Let's begin with the step-by-step approach I most recommend for crafters. Using the sample Mallorca necklace from Chapter 4, here's a summary of what we'll do:

1. Quantify costs.

2. Use a pricing formula to estimate a "working" wholesale price range.

3. Use the working wholesale price range to estimate a retail price range.

4. Use market factors to narrow down the retail price range.

5. Use the retail price to determine actual wholesale price.

In the end, we'll have a pretty good idea of how to price the necklace for retail and wholesale. I'll note the retail price on both my product information sheet and my finished goods information list.

Quantifying Costs

There are two types of costs relevant to pricing: direct costs and indirect costs. Direct costs are the unique costs of making a finished good. They include the cost of raw materials and labor. Indirect costs are the same as overhead costs, which are general expenses that you incur no matter which finished goods you make. Once you quantify all these costs, you can plug them into pricing formulas.

Cost of Raw Materials

You can find your cost of raw materials on your item's product information sheet. On the Mallorca necklace product information sheet in Chapter 4, I determined that my total cost of raw material components (based on average cost per unit) was $24.79.

Cost of Labor

Your product information sheet also indicates the time you spent on design and assembly, which you use to calculate your estimated cost of labor. You need a cost of labor for accurate pricing even though you don't actually give yourself a paycheck.

Ideally, your cost of labor should be a fair market wage for your work. It should be higher if you're expertly skilled or your crafting process is complicated and lower if you're a novice or your process is pretty simple. Many crafters use between about $10 and $30 per hour. You can better dial yours in by asking other crafters in your craft medium what figure they use.

Hitting a Snag

Don't confuse the method you use for pricing with the records you keep in your bookkeeping journals. When you set prices, it's okay to use loose estimates. When you keep books, you must record numbers as precisely as possible and save receipts or other documents that back them up.

For the Mallorca necklace, my total design and assembly time was 1 hour and 30 minutes. Because this is a simple necklace made from stock beads and strung on cable, I'll set my cost of labor at a reasonable $12 per hour.

But there's something else to consider. As noted on my product information sheet, this necklace is a limited edition that I plan to copy up to 30 times. Each copy after the first needs to be assembled but not designed. How should I value the one hour of design time for the first copy? A good approach is to allocate a portion of it to all copies. I don't know how many copies I'll ultimately make (only that they won't exceed 30), but I'm pretty sure I'll make at least five. Based on that estimate, here's how I can set a cost of labor.

1 hour = 60 minutes

60 minutes of design time ÷ 5 copies = 12 minutes of design time per copy

30 minutes of assembly time + 12 minutes of design time = 42 minutes of total labor per copy

$12 per hour ÷ 60 minutes = 20¢ per minute

$0.20 × 42 minutes = $8.40 cost of labor per copy

Notice that because my cost of labor is spread out over several copies, it's lower than if I had planned to make only one copy. This is the main reason why you can price stock and limited edition designs below one-of-a-kind designs.

Other Direct Costs

Occasionally, you may have other direct costs apart from raw materials and labor. For example, if you drive a long way to purchase unique components for a design, you might treat your cost of gasoline as a direct cost. When you incorporate incidental ingredients such as glue or glitter in a design, you can also treat them as estimated direct costs.

Overhead Costs

Overhead costs are typically measured over a set period time, such as one year. Once you've been selling for a while, you can estimate them based on data from past years—but when you're just getting started, you need to make an estimate. Your goal is to come up with a cost figure that you can allocate to the prices of your finished goods.

As a starting point, many crafters estimate overhead costs as a percentage of an item's direct costs. Typical overhead percentages range from about 10 to 20 percent. If you're a casual seller, the lower figure is probably more accurate.

Here's what the overhead cost formula looks like:

cost of raw materials + cost of labor = direct cost = X

10 percent of X = overhead cost

Accordingly, here's how I can estimate my overhead cost allocation for the Mallorca necklace:

$X = \$24.79 + \$8.40 = \$33.19$

overhead cost $= 0.10 \times \$33.19 = \$3.32$

Honing overhead costs beyond this estimate is tricky because some costs depend on how many sales you actually make. For example, you're charged certain sales venue and payment processing fees only when an item sells. If you become a more active seller, you can use your bookkeeping records to estimate sales numbers—and therefore general overhead costs—more accurately.

Using Pricing Formulas

Once you have cost figures, you can use them in pricing formulas. Begin by totaling your direct and indirect costs to determine your *minimum price*. Then use a formula to add to—or mark up—that price to generate some profit.

Term Tag

Minimum price is the price that covers your costs but does not generate a profit. From a business perspective, it's typically the lowest price you should charge. You can think of it as your "break-even" point.

Calculating Minimum Price

Here's my minimum price calculation for the Mallorca necklace:

direct costs (raw materials + labor):	$32.39
indirect costs (overhead):	+ $3.32
minimum price:	$35.71

If I had incurred another direct cost, such as the cost of incidentals, I would include it in my total direct costs along with raw materials and labor—making my minimum price slightly higher.

Wholesale Pricing Formula

Once you know your minimum price, you can use a formula to help you set a working wholesale price or price range. I call this a "working" price because it's not the ultimate wholesale price you use if you decide to sell to resellers; it's only for help calculating your retail price. You'll see what I mean in the next section.

Here's a traditional wholesale pricing formula:

minimum price + profit = retail price

"Profit" in the formula is the amount of profit you can reasonably expect to make when you sell an item. For crafts, it's typically somewhere between 10 percent and 100 percent of your minimum price. To narrow that down, you may need to do some experimental sales and learn more about the market. For now, I recommend that you use both extremes to define a range of potential prices. Later in this chapter, I'll help you refine it by considering other pricing factors.

Hitting a Snag

Don't confuse your profit with your taxable income. The entire price of each item sold is included in the gross income that you report on your income tax return. Depending on your situation, you might be able to deduct your costs of materials and incidentals but not the cost of your own labor.

Using this approach, here's how I can calculate a wholesale price range for the Mallorca necklace:

low end (10 percent profit): $35.71 + ($35.71 × 0.10) = $39.28

high end (100 percent profit): $35.71 + ($35.71 × 1) = $71.42

Rounding these numbers off, my working wholesale price range is about $40 to $70.

Retail Pricing Formula

The traditional retail formula involves simply doubling your wholesale price. If I double my working wholesale prices for the necklace, I end up with a range of $80 to $140 retail:

low end: $40 × 2 = $80

high end: $70 × 2 = $140

If I'm curious about my profit margin, or percentage profit, on the necklace at retail, I can calculate it by subtracting the minimum price:

low end:

$80 - $35.71 = $44.29 (rounded to $45)

100([$45 ÷ $80]) = 56 percent profit

high end:

$140 - $35.71 = $104.29 (rounded to $105)

100([$105 ÷ $140]) = 75 percent profit

Narrowing Down Price Ranges

You should try to price your goods at their optimum price point, which is the price at which they are in highest demand while still generating a profit. Of course, it's hard to know for sure what that price is. With a little thought, however, you can at least come close. Start by narrowing down your retail price range.

Researching the Retail Market

Look for clues to what customers are willing to pay by assessing what other successful sellers charge for similar goods. By successful, I mean sellers whose products routinely sell—not other beginners testing the water. You can do this online by browsing shopping sites that provide sales data. For example, on the website Etsy.com, the number of sales that a seller has made appears on each shop's home page. You can even click through to see which products are especially popular.

If you plan to sell in person, visit shops and craft shows and take note of the prices on items that receive a lot of attention from customers. You can also ask other craft sellers about their prices. Many are willing to share advice.

To make the best use of your research, make lists and keep notes about the prices you find. Here's a hypothetical list for the Mallorca necklace:

Pricing Research: Necklaces Similar to Mallorca Necklace

	Date: 02/06/10		
Venue	**Seller/Crafter**	**Price**	**Notes**
Etsy	Sophia Nex	$55	Necklace very similar, and seller is popular
Etsy	Deneuge Gems	$64	Necklace uses white quartz, not onyx
Artfire	Ula's Stash	$39	Quality questionable
K Boutique	Darla Smith	$70	Comes with free stud earrings

So how do I use this information? I know from running formulas that my target retail price is between about $45 and $105. The market prices on my research list range from $39 to $70. Taken together, these suggest that I should price the necklace somewhere between $45 (my low) and $70 (the highest market price) retail.

I can use my notes to narrow that down even more. First, I'll exclude the $39 necklace, because it's below my preferred low price and its quality wasn't great. Next, I'll look at the highest-priced necklace. It was for sale in an upscale boutique and included a "free" pair of earrings. Because I plan to sell the necklace online and I'm not including a free gift, I'll scratch that one off the list, too. That leaves me with two comparisons: $55 and $64. At this point, I might go back and do more market research to confirm whether these are in the ball park.

Other Pricing Considerations

Finally, try to identify any special factors that might raise or lower the demand for your crafts. For example:

♦ Are your products part of a new fashion or style trend?

♦ Are your raw materials more desirable to your target customers than most of your competitors' materials?

♦ Have you received any special media attention, such as a feature story in a local newspaper or magazine?

♦ How popular is your craft medium among other craft sellers? That is, how much direct competition do you face?

♦ What's the status of the economy, and how is it affecting your target customers?

For instance, I plan to sell the Mallorca necklace in a slightly down economy where my target customers are a bit hesitant to spend. I also have lots of competition from other crafters who make beaded jewelry. These challenges suggest a lower price for the necklace.

 Bits and Pieces

In the United States, it's common to see "odd prices," where an item is marked one or a few cents below the next round dollar (for example, $9.99 rather than $10) in an effort to make the price appear lower. You may want to avoid this with your crafts, however, because the appearance of lower prices can be mistaken for lower quality. Rounded prices also make it easier to make change when you sell in person for cash.

On the other hand, the necklace's pendant is a rare style that should greatly appeal to my target customers, and some of my designs were recently featured in a magazine that my target customers read. These benefits might allow me to price the necklace a little higher.

Ultimately, the exact retail price you choose is up to you. Do what you think is best based on all the information you have. With crafts, it's often worthwhile to use the higher end of your price range, rather than the low end or middle. Depending on your craft medium, your target customers, your venue, and other factors, you may benefit from prestige pricing—where goods are perceived as being more valuable because of their high price. Higher initial prices also allow you to lower your prices over time without taking a loss.

Establishing Wholesale Discounts

Once you have a retail price, you can do simple math to refine your wholesale price range. Recall that when you sell wholesale, you offer resellers a discount on your retail prices in exchange for bulk purchases. The simplest approach is to set a minimum wholesale order amount and offer a percentage discount.

Traditionally, resellers preferred to buy goods at 50 percent of their retail prices (and mark them up 100 percent to resell). However, in order to justify a discount as large as 50 percent, a wholesale order must be pretty large—larger than what many crafters and craft resellers want to commit to. A solution is to set a more reasonable minimum order amount and offer a slightly lower discount, such as 25 or 30 percent.

Your minimum wholesale order amount can be either in dollar terms or in volume. For instance, you might offer either a 30 percent discount on a minimum purchase of 25 items or a 30 percent discount on a minimum purchase of $300.

Either way, the discount is always subtracted from the total retail price. However, when you use a dollar amount to define a minimum purchase, you need to decide whether it refers to a total of the goods' retail prices or their effective wholesale prices after the discount is taken. A 30 percent discount on $300 at retail results in a wholesale order of $210 for goods valued at $300 retail, whereas the same discount at wholesale results in an order of $300 for goods valued at about $429 (because $300 is $429 less 30 percent).

Some crafters use tiered wholesale pricing: they offer smaller discounts for smaller orders and larger discounts for larger ones. Whether and how you devise tiers is up to you. It depends on how important wholesale orders are to you and how much profit you want to make from them.

Let's say that I offer the following tiered wholesale discounts:

Minimum Order (Retail Prices)	Discount
$300	20 percent
$350	25 percent
$400	30 percent

Accordingly, if I decide to set a retail price of $64 for the Mallorca necklace, then its wholesale price would range between 70 percent and 80 percent of $64, or between about $45 and $51.

As a final check, I'll compare this price range with the working $40-to-$70 wholesale price range that I generated earlier (using the wholesale pricing formula). Because my final wholesale range fits within it, I know that I'll still make a profit—even with the discounts.

If my lowest wholesale price had been lower than $40 (the low end of my working range), then I might still decide to sell at that price as long as it remained somewhat higher than my minimum price of about $36. Otherwise, I wouldn't even cover my costs. I would need to either increase retail price (to pull up the wholesale price) or reduce my wholesale discount percentages—and, optionally, my minimum wholesale order amounts.

Fine-Tuning Your Prices

If you'd like to try increasing your profit, you can adjust your prices over time. Keep a record of these adjustments and their dates so that you can compare "before" and "after" sales figures later.

Although you should avoid significant price increases (which can scare off customers), it's usually safe to raise them incrementally. Some crafters make more sales after raising their prices because of the benefits of prestige pricing. Others experience a drop in sales, confirming that their previous prices were more in line with the market.

To find out whether you overestimated what most of your target customers are willing to pay, you can try lowering prices. However, I recommend that you only keep them lowered if that results in more sales. If it doesn't, pricing is probably not your problem, and you should consider making other changes.

Bits and Pieces

You can lower prices temporarily by holding sales and offering discount coupons. These can be great for promotion, but their value in assessing prices is limited. That's because temporary sales and specials generate excitement that induces customers to make purchases they might not otherwise make—even if regular prices were lower.

Reducing Costs

Whether or not you decide to change your prices, always keep an eye out for ways to increase profit by reducing costs without sacrificing quality or value. Here are some possibilities:

- Find better deals on raw materials and general supplies (which might include negotiating prices downward or buying in bulk).

- Substitute more complicated techniques with less time-consuming ones.

- Switch to a more affordable, but still appropriate, sales venue.

- Substitute certain handmade components in your products with commercially made components (being careful not to disappoint your target customers).

- Offer more stock or limited edition designs and fewer (or no) one-of-a-kind designs.

- Eliminate or reduce wasteful costs, such as ineffective advertising or business services that offer more than you really need.

Other Ways to Increase Sales

If your sales are slower than you'd like, there are other methods for increasing them besides lowering prices. You can improve your product packaging and displays (see Chapter 6), make your business policies more customer friendly (see Chapter 7), or enhance your promotional techniques (see Chapter 8).

Pricing for Multiple Channels or Venues

Be aware that prices appropriate for one sales channel or venue may be too high or too low to work well in others. This is important if you want to sell in multiple channels or venues. Fortunately, you should be able to identify price-point discrepancies through a little research. For instance, you might find that some crafts are consistently priced lower online than they are at craft shows. That's an important clue that the two channels target different customers (at least for that craft medium), so you should probably choose one or the other but not both.

If you do take the plunge into multiple sales channels or venues, do what you can to keep prices as close as possible among them. Customers who pay higher prices will feel cheated if they find out about lower prices—unless their purchase was somehow more valuable. Try adding value at higher-price venues by offering free gifts, upgraded packaging, or extra services such as free customization with each purchase. And when you sell to resellers, do your best to keep from undercutting the retail prices they plan to charge for the same items. We'll revisit that issue in Chapter 18.

SOLD Selling Secrets

One of the benefits of being an indie crafter is that you can price your goods just about any way you like. If you don't need or want to make a profit, there's technically nothing stopping you from setting prices at or even below cost. But if you go that route, be prepared for resistance from the crafting community. Some craft sellers, especially those who are more active, shun sellers who underprice. They believe that underpricing leads to decreased sales for all crafters. Consider this when you set prices.

Pricing for Custom Orders

With a custom order, you typically provide a customer with a price quote based on the design they have requested. Because you haven't crafted the item yet, you need to estimate which raw materials you'll use and the total time you'll devote to design and assembly. You can then use those estimates to work through your regular pricing process. If your price comes out higher than the customer would like to pay, discuss with them ways you can lower it, such as by switching out raw materials or simplifying the design.

The Least You Need to Know

- The minimum price that you charge for an item should cover its direct and indirect costs.

- Estimate your cost of labor by assigning yourself a fair hourly wage.

- You can use a percentage of your direct costs to estimate your overhead costs.

- Begin estimating prices by using wholesale and retail formulas, then refine those estimates based on market factors.

- To increase sales, you can try lowering or raising prices or altering your selling strategies to make your goods more marketable.

Chapter 6

Creating an Identity

In This Chapter

◆ Selecting a seller name

◆ Marketing with color

◆ Logo options

◆ Packaging, tagging, and labeling your wares

You can sell more crafts by creating and maintaining an identity that customers remember. In business-speak, this is called brand identity. You establish it by doing whatever you can to demonstrate your style and set a mood for your crafts. In this chapter, we look at how your seller name, marketing materials, displays, tags, labels, and packaging all play important roles in enforcing your brand identity.

What's in a Name?

As a one-person operation, your full name is the legal name of your business. But you can also use an assumed, or doing-business-as (DBA), seller name—as long as you comply with business name laws and select a name that's not already in use.

How a Seller Name Communicates Style

Your seller name can subtly introduce your customers to your crafting style. For example, because people often associate personal names with fine artwork, I might use the name Chris Franchetti Michaels as my seller name if my jewelry is all one of a kind or limited edition. But if I carry lots of casual, stock designs, I might select a more creative name that's easier to remember, such as The Beaded Mockingbird.

To see how other crafters select and use seller names, browse online shopping websites and look around at craft shows. Although you can't copy anyone's name, you can at least get a feel for the moods that different names create.

Selecting an Unused Name

If you decide to use an assumed name, it's important for trademark and other legal reasons to select one that's not already in use. Search the Internet for the name you're considering, using it as a search term ("seller name") and in URLs (such as "www.*sellername*.com") with all the possible domain suffixes (.com, .net, .info, .us, and so on). You can also perform an online trademark search, such as the one available on the U.S. Copyright and Trademark website (www.uspto.gov). If you discover that a crafter is already using the name, discard it and try another. If a noncrafter is using it, discard it unless an attorney advises you otherwise.

Fictitious Business Names

Even as a casual seller, you need to comply with state or local laws that govern assumed names. If you live in the United States, visit the website www.business.gov for a list of these laws by state.

Many jurisdictions require you to file a fictitious business name, or trade name, before you start selling under an assumed name. These filings typically involve completing an application and paying a fee. As part of the process, a records check confirms whether the name is available in your locality. If your name is approved, you may be required to publish a notice in a local newspaper to complete the filing. Your business name then becomes part of the public record.

Presenting Your Seller Name

Once you settle on a name, decide how best to present it to potential customers. When you print your name on materials such as business cards and craft show banners, its very appearance—the way it's written and the color of the text—should invoke your brand identity.

SOLD **Selling Secrets** _____

The word-processing program on your computer probably includes a collection of font styles. Type your seller name using each one. If nothing strikes your fancy, search online for other fonts that you can download and install, making sure that their copyright permissions allow for commercial use.

Selecting a Marketing Color Scheme

Colors are valuable tools for creating a mood and establishing your identity. Select one or more colors to use consistently in your displays and on business cards, tags, labels, and websites. Make sure they are easy to reproduce and consistent with your style. A graphic designer can advise you about which colors work best in print and online; try posting your questions in online forums where these experts are likely to spend time.

Using a Logo

A logo is a visual representation of your brand that helps potential customers remember and recognize your crafts. It can be a simple, stylized letter of the alphabet or an intricate, multicolor graphic.

Logos are handy for promotion and are generally fun to use. However, it takes some work to establish one. You must come up with a design that accurately reflects your style, do your best to make sure that it's not being used by someone else, and figure out how to present it in a professional manner. Fortunately, logos are completely optional for crafters. Feel free to skip one if it's more than you'd like to take on.

If you do decide to use a logo, you can design it yourself using graphics software, hire a logo designer, or purchase a premade logo online. Alternatively, you might use a combination approach, where you sketch out your logo idea and hire a graphic artist to finalize it. Ask other crafter sellers for logo design recommendations. You can often find independent graphics artists who offer reasonable prices on shopping sites such as Etsy.com. If you hire someone, ask for your finished logo in several useful sizes and in a proper format for printing.

Hitting a Snag

It can be very difficult to confirm that a logo design—or one similar to it—isn't already in use by someone else. To avoid potential trademark problems, get creative with your logo and make it as unique as you can. If you hire a logo designer, they should ensure that the logo they create for you is completely original.

Putting On a Display

When you sell in person, you display your wares by setting them out to be viewed and examined by potential customers.

Your display is often a shopper's first impression of your work—especially if your goods are small and difficult to see from a distance. It should encourage people to walk over and take a look. And once customers are looking, your display can add to or detract from the perceived value of your crafts.

The Best Presentation for Your Crafts

Make it a goal to design your display in a way that makes your goods appear as valuable as possible. You can find lots of display ideas online and in magazines, but they won't all be the best choices for your crafts. Focus on what attracts and engages your target customers.

Start by gathering some fabrics and accessories that coordinate with your color scheme and thinking about how you can use them to enhance your display area (usually a table top). Keep things simple; too much detail or busyness detracts from your crafts. Remember that your crafts themselves must ultimately win the attention of shoppers.

Your price range plays a role in how you should set up your display. Relatively low-priced goods can be grouped closely together to emphasize the variety that you have available. But you should display pricier goods separately, and space them more sparsely, to showcase their uniqueness and heightened value.

Making Display Props

Many crafters save money by constructing their own display props, such as stands, risers, and shelves. You can find tips and instructions for a wide range of display projects online. You can also repurpose items that you find at thrift stores or online auction sites and modify them to match your color scheme and style. Just make sure that your completed props have a professional look and feel; spend the time necessary to make them worthy of your crafts.

Tagging Your Wares

Customers love hang tags. They give your goods a more personalized feel and an appearance of increased value. And they have the added benefit of helping customers remember who you are in case they'd like to buy from you again.

Making Your Own Hang Tags

You can make distinctive hang tags using scrapbooking supplies such as these:

- ◆ Sheets or precut shapes of card stock
- ◆ Calligraphy and scrapbooking pens
- ◆ Glue, pigments, and glitter
- ◆ Brads, grommets, and eyelets
- ◆ Stamps and ink pads
- ◆ Decorative paper (for layering on card stock)
- ◆ Lightweight charms

- Hole punches in various sizes and shapes

- Paper-cutting die machines and trimmers

- Stencils

These supplies are typically sold at craft stores. If you need help using them, read a good scrapbooking book or magazine for tips. Alternatively, you can make tags on your computer using design software and a color printer. Print them onto light card stock and cut them out yourself, or buy printable, precut business cards to cut or fold into hang tags. Use a hole punch to pierce the corners or edges of your tags and tie them to your goods with ribbon, embroidery thread, or—if your crafts are more rustic—jute or hemp twine. With fabric goods, you can attach tags with small safety pins.

Other Low-Cost Tagging Solutions

You can also design tags online using websites that specialize in card printing. These typically give you the option of selecting a design from a premade collection or uploading your own. You can create business cards that become tags when you cut or fold them, or hire a company such as MOO (us.moo.com) to print your tags in a smaller size.

What to Include on Tags

At a minimum, your tags should display your seller name and demonstrate your color scheme. If you have enough space, you can also include contact information, such as your e-mail address, website, or phone number.

When you sell in person, I also recommend that you include prices on your tags, because most customers appreciate the ability to learn prices without having to ask. If you prefer that prices remain hidden when your goods are on display, make a point of keeping tags turned face up, with the prices on the backs, so that customers can still check them.

Bits and Pieces _____

Consider using small, removable stickers to attach prices to tags so that you can easily remove them when you make sales or need to change prices. However, always keep a list of your actual prices on hand (preferably as part of your finished goods inventory list) to confirm the accuracy of price stickers.

Labeling Your Goods

Labels can include the same types of information that tags do, but they're especially useful for listing ingredients or directions.

You can use labels in place of tags if your goods aren't well suited for tagging. For example, it might be easier to stick a label on a jar of body lotion than to hang a tag from it.

You can use labels to communicate your brand identity, just as you would with tags. But some labels are required by law. These are informative labels that provide, at minimum, lists of ingredients or raw materials. Whether you're required to use them depends on your craft medium and the laws in place where you live. Targeted goods can include textiles, edibles, lotions, cosmetics, and items for children. See the Supplemental Appendix at www.craftychannels.com/resources for some resources to help you research whether these rules apply to your crafts and how to comply with them.

Hitting a Snag _____

Be aware that it may be illegal to make certain claims about your crafts on tags and labels. For example, a U.S. Federal Trade Commission law prohibits claiming that an item was made in the U.S.A. (or made "in America") unless almost all of its components—including raw materials—were manufactured in the United States.

Stickers work well as labels for solid goods with smooth surfaces. You can design your own on your computer and print them onto blank sticker sheets from an office supply store or order them through an online printing service.

Many crafters label their textiles using sewn-in or ironed-on (fused) strips of sturdy fabric, fabric tape, or premade fabric labels. You can find blank fabric labels at many fabric stores for writing on using a permanent marker. For more professional results, you can create your own label designs, print them onto inkjet-printable fabric from a craft store, cut them out, and sew them in. Or, you can order custom labels from a fabric-label supplier on the Internet.

Pretty Packages

The materials you use to package sold goods play an important role in creating your brand identity. Use your imagination to develop a unique packaging style that impresses your target customers. Consider using gift boxes, bags or pouches, ribbon, strings, tissue paper, scrapbooking charms, paper confetti, and more. You can find these supplies online or at larger craft stores.

If possible, secure packaging to your crafts in a way that allows it to be removed and replaced, or opened and closed, without damage. For example, if you use jewelry boxes, you might secure them with colored elastic string rather than ribbon. This allows customers to inspect items before giving them as gifts with the packaging intact.

Take advantage of opportunities to display your packaging at sales venues. When you sell in person, keep sample packages in clear view on your table (they can be empty because they're only for show). If you sell online, include stylish photos of your packaging in sales listings.

The Least You Need to Know

- Create a brand identity to attract your target customers and help repeat customers remember you.

- Select a seller name that communicates your crafting style.

- Settle on a color scheme to use in all your marketing materials, in your displays, and on websites.

- Try using logos, displays, tags, labels, and packaging to build and maintain your brand identity.

7

Developing Business Policies and Practices

In This Chapter

♦ Making payment and shipping decisions

♦ Accepting returns and offering guarantees

♦ Other policy considerations

This chapter is about making rules that help you strike a balance between keeping your customers happy and minimizing your risks. These rules fall into two categories: policies, which you communicate to all of your customers; and practices, which you keep private.

Your policies govern the forms of payment you accept, how you ship orders (if you sell online), and whether you accept returns or make guarantees. Your practices control how you respond to situations not specifically addressed by your policies. You'll use both types of rules from the moment you start selling, and you can update them over time.

Because you openly share your policies, you need to write them in a clear, organized manner for potential customers to read. You may also choose to write down your practices for your own reference. Take a moment now to review the appendix for some examples.

Forms of Payment

There are benefits and risks to consider with all forms of payment. Choose to accept the ones you feel most comfortable with.

Cash

Although cash is relatively safe to accept in person, it's risky to receive by mail because it cannot be accurately tracked or canceled by the customer if lost. For this reason, many crafters choose not to accept cash for online orders.

Checks

Checks are promises to pay in the future from a customer's checking account. Before you can receive actual payment from a check, you must deposit it into your own bank account and wait for it to clear. If a customer's account is overdrawn or a check was stolen, not only will you not get paid but your own bank may also charge you a fee (called a returned check fee) for depositing a bad check.

If you decide to accept checks, it's a good idea to adopt some or all of the following practices to help lower your risk:

 ◆ **Confirm the customer's identity.** When you sell in person, you can require that the information on each check matches the name, address, and phone number on the customer's driver's license or identification card. Write down that information, along with the license or I.D. number, on your copy of each sales receipt. You can use it later to contact the customer or to assist the bank or law enforcement if the check is reported as stolen.

- **Verify checks with the issuing bank.** If you have access to a phone at your sales venue, you can call the bank to confirm that a checking account is not overdrawn. Dial the customer service number and explain that you'd like to verify funds drawn on one of the bank's accounts. If the account has insufficient funds or the check is reported as stolen, courteously refuse the check and explain the situation to the customer.

Bits and Pieces

Occasionally, a customer may question you for checking their I.D. or calling their bank. Be honest and explain that in addition to protecting yourself, you want to protect them from potential identity theft or unauthorized use of their checking account.

- **Don't ship an online order until a check clears.** Because checks can take between one and two weeks to clear, be sure to alert customers of this delay in your policies. To minimize it, deposit checks right away and monitor your account to find out when they clear.

- **Cap the amount that you accept by check.** You can limit your financial risk by accepting checks only up to a certain value, such as $50 or $100. Require customers to use a more reliable method—such as cash or a payment processor such as PayPal—for larger orders.

- **Charge a fee for returned checks.** Your policies can state that you charge a fee for bounced checks as reimbursement for the fee that your bank charges you. This policy may dissuade people from knowingly writing bad checks. However, keep in mind that it can be difficult to collect returned check fees because you need to contact the customer (who may have given you false contact information) and convince him or her to pay your penalty—preferably using a method other than a check.

Money Orders and Cashier's Checks

Because customers pay up front when they purchase a money order or cashier's check, these documents cannot bounce the way regular checks can. However, they can still be stolen or counterfeited, so it's a good idea to wait for them to clear before you ship.

Credit Cards

To accept credit cards in person, you typically need what's called a merchant account for processing credit card numbers. Merchant accounts require substantial commitment and add a layer of responsibility to selling. We'll cover them in Chapter 12.

Fortunately, accepting credit cards online is relatively easy because you can use an online payment processor that processes them on your behalf. Popular options include PayPal (www.paypal.com), Google Checkout (checkout.google.com), and 2checkout.com. Depending on which service you use, customers may need to sign up with the payment processor before making a payment. Because this can discourage some customers from completing their orders, you should avoid using service plans that require it when possible.

Hitting a Snag

Most payment processors and merchant account providers do not allow you to charge customers a fee to cover the fees they charge you. Instead, you need to treat these as overhead and include them in your prices.

As I mentioned in Chapter 1, online payment processors usually charge a small fee for each transaction they process. The money they collect from your customers (less that fee) is credited to your account, which is much like a bank account. You can transfer money from your payment processor account to your real bank account or use it for other purposes.

Whether you accept payment through a merchant account or an online payment processor, there's always a risk of fraud. Your merchant account provider or payment processor will ask you to follow guidelines that help lower this risk. But even without fraud, you may occasionally receive a chargeback, or payment reversal, from a customer. This can happen if a customer fails to receive his or her order or is unhappy with his or her purchase. As with bounced checks, you may be charged a fee for chargebacks. You can try to avoid them by communicating openly with your customers and accepting returns.

Payment Deadlines

Although it's standard business practice to require immediate payment for in-person orders, many shopping and auction sites allow customers to order now and pay later. If you use those sites, you need a policy that sets a deadline for payment. When you don't receive payment by the deadline, you may decide to cancel the order—but it's a good idea to attempt to contact the customer first to see whether he or she has questions or concerns.

General Shipping Policies

If you sell online, your policies and practices should describe when and where you ship orders.

When to Ship

Indicate a time frame within which you normally ship after payment clears. It should be reasonable for both you and your customers. Be sure to give yourself more time for made-to-order designs because you'll need time to craft them.

Shipping to Matching Addresses

Sometimes when you accept payment by credit card or through an online payment processor, a customer requests that you ship to a different address than the card issuer or payment processor has on file. Many craft sellers make it a policy to ship only to the address on file, which is called shipping to a "matching address." This makes it less convenient for customers to purchase gifts (because they can't ship directly to recipients), but it can protect you from unwittingly accepting fraudulent payment.

International Shipping

You may or may not decide to ship outside your own country. Doing so usually results in more sales, but it also introduces these inconveniences:

- **International shipping insurance can be expensive, and may even be unavailable.** Without insurance, you and the customer have no recourse if a package is lost in the mail.

- **Tracking may be unavailable.** This is often the case when you ship internationally through the postal service, making it impossible to confirm whether a package was delivered.

- **You may need to fill out and submit customs forms.** This depends on the package's contents, weight, and destination country. You can check with your country's postal service to find out when a customs form is required. Keep in mind that the U.S. Postal Service typically requires that you hand packages with customs forms to a postal employee rather than dropping them into a collection box.

- **Customers may be charged additional fees when their packages arrive.** This happens in countries where tariffs or customs fees apply to your goods. Fees are normally based on the value of the goods, which you enter on the customs form.

Bits and Pieces

Occasionally, a customer may request you to write "gift" or "sample" on a customs form so that a package appears to be exempt from fees. However, this is illegal when a package contains a commercial order that is otherwise subject to those fees. I recommend making it a practice to courteously refuse such requests.

- **International orders are more likely to be fraudulent than domestic orders.** You can limit this risk by researching which countries are most commonly associated with fraudulent orders and making it a policy not to ship to them. But you should also use common sense: as a practice, cancel any large international orders that seem suspicious. When in doubt, ask for advice from other craft sellers.

Carrier Options

You can ship orders via the postal service or through a private carrier, such as UPS or FedEx.

Using the Postal Service

In the United States, there are several options for buying postage. The traditional method is to take your packages to the post office, stand in line at the counter, and ask a postal clerk to weigh them and affix their postage. But you may find it easier to use one of the newer, automated kiosks in post office lobbies or print your own postage using your computer.

> **SOLD** | **Selling Secrets**
>
> In the United States, antiterrorism laws prohibit depositing any stamped package that weighs more than 13 ounces into a collection box. Instead, you must hand those packages to a postal employee. Postage printed online or at a post office kiosk is exempt from this rule.

Automated postage kiosks weigh packages, calculate postage, charge your credit card, and print self-stick postage labels. Most post offices keep a large collection box nearby for depositing packages once you have paid for and labeled them.

Alternatively, you can weigh your own packages and buy and print postage online using the postal service website. Some online payment processors and shopping sites also allow you to buy and print postage through them. You can print postage labels onto regular paper, cut them out, and tape them to your packages or purchase blank postage label stickers from an office supply store.

Under some circumstances, the postal service may offer free pickup of packages from your home, saving you a trip to the post office if you print postage from your computer. When this book was written, free next-day pickup was available for Priority Mail but not for First Class (see the next section). Check with the postal service for updated terms and conditions.

Postal Service Shipping Methods

The U.S. Postal Service offers three basic levels of shipping for packages: Parcel Post, First Class, and Priority Mail. Parcel Post is the most affordable, but it can have long delivery times, especially if you ship to a distant location. Only use this option when your customer is content with waiting well over a week for delivery. First Class is a faster method, with a typical delivery time of two to four days, but it's only available for packages with a maximum weight of 13 ounces. Heavier packages can ship by Priority Mail, which is pricier but includes a free mailer or box and guarantees delivery within a few days.

The postal service also offers some express shipping options, such as overnight delivery, but they're somewhat limited and can be more expensive than similar services from private carriers.

Using a Private Carrier

For large, heavy, or perishable orders, you may find it economical to use a private carrier. Much like the postal service, these carriers allow you to purchase and print labels online, and you can either drop off your packages or pay an extra fee to have them picked up. Private shippers also offer free packaging materials to use with their services.

Private Carrier Shipping Methods

Ground shipping is the most affordable, and slowest, private carrier shipping method. Ground packages often take a week or more to arrive. Faster methods include three-day, two-day, and overnight delivery. Because these express options are all relatively expensive, you should use them only upon customer request or for perishable goods that must arrive quickly.

Bits and Pieces

You can order the free mailers and boxes provided for select shipping methods through each carrier's website. However, only use them with their indicated shipping methods. Most carriers' terms and conditions prohibit using their free boxes with other, less expensive shipping methods by turning them inside out. And when it comes to the postal service, doing so can be a violation of federal law.

Shipping Guarantees and Special Services

Your shipping policies should indicate who assumes the risk for packages after you ship them. Special services such as tracking and shipping insurance can make that risk more manageable.

Lost, Damaged, or Stolen Packages

You have options for dealing with packages that are lost, damaged, or stolen in transit. The most customer-friendly option is to guarantee safe delivery of all packages; that is, when something goes awry, you provide the customer with a full refund or replacement. With this approach, it's your choice whether to purchase shipping insurance to cover your risk.

If you'd rather not guarantee safe delivery, you might give customers the option of purchasing their own insurance for a fee. Be aware, however, that some online sales venues do not permit this approach.

The least customer-friendly option is to decline responsibility for shipped packages and inform customers that no insurance is available. This is not a standard business practice for selling crafts, and it can scare off potential customers.

Tracking Packages

When you guarantee safe shipping or your customer buys insurance, you should use a tracking service that records a package's delivery date. For a small fee, the U.S. Postal Service offers Delivery Confirmation, where packages are scanned upon delivery. Private carriers usually include tracking with their services for no additional fee. With most carriers, you can check delivery status or track packages online using the carrier's website.

Insurance Claims

Shipping insurance covers the value of goods that are damaged or lost in the mail. You can order insurance through the postal service, your private carrier, or a third-party insurance provider on the Internet.

To recover a loss, you or your customer must file an insurance claim. Each insurance plan has its own rules for accepting and processing claims, but most require that you meet certain conditions to qualify for reimbursement. Here are some typical examples:

◆ You must provide proof of damage or nondelivery.

◆ The goods must have been packaged securely, in a sturdy container and with adequate cushioning material.

◆ The package must have been clearly and correctly labeled.

◆ The package must not have contained prohibited substances, such as liquids.

◆ You must provide proof of the value of the goods, such as a sales receipt.

◆ If a package is lost, you may need to wait at least 21 days after shipment before filing a claim.

◆ Insurance may not cover packages that are lost or stolen after delivery.

Keep in mind that if an insurance claim is refused because a condition is not met, you may need to personally reimburse the customer.

Covering Shipping Costs

Your shipping costs generally include carrier fees (for postage or private carrier services), the cost of packaging materials, and the cost of labor involved in preparing orders for shipment. Your policies or practices should address how you cover them.

Dealing with Carrier Fees

You can either treat carrier fees as overhead and include them in your prices or charge them to customers as separate fees. The overhead approach allows you to label goods as having free shipping, which attracts certain types of customers—but charging separate fees lets you set slightly lower prices. Use the approach that your target customers will most likely prefer.

Charging for Shipping

If you charge fees for shipping, it's usually easiest to make them flat fees based on estimates of your actual shipping costs. Here's an approach to setting them:

1. Estimate the typical weights of packages that you'll ship (including the weight of packaging materials) for orders of single items. If your packages will vary in size and weight, make a range of estimates.

2. Check carrier fee charts to determine the costs of shipping those packages to various locations using your preferred shipping method and any special services that you plan to use.

3. Optionally, estimate the cost of shipping materials for each package and add it to the carrier fees.

Using this method, I might create the following chart to help me set fees for orders shipped within the United States:

Sample Shipping Fee Chart

Package Weight	Shipping Method	Carrier (USPS) Fees	Estimated Cost of Materials	Total	My Shipping Fee
1oz–4 oz	First Class	$1.22–$1.73	$0.55	$1.77–$2.28	$2.00
5oz–9oz	First Class	$1.90–2.58	$0.95	$2.85–$3.53	$3.25
10oz–13oz	First Class	$2.75–3.26	$0.95	$3.70–$4.21	$4.00
14oz +	Priority Mail	$4.95–$11.00	$0.45	$5.40–$11.45	$8.50

Sample shipping fees based on cost estimates.

Notice that my weights, and therefore my carrier fees, are ranges that I'm using as package categories to simplify my results. To set my shipping fees (in the last column), I guessed where most of my packages would fall within each range and rounded to the nearest quarter dollar. If I keep track of my actual shipments and shipping costs over time, I can change my fees if they turn out to be too high or low.

You should also decide how to charge shipping for orders that contain more than one item, because shipping items together often costs less than shipping them separately. For instance, you might charge a smaller flat fee for each additional item or simply ship those items for free. If you charge a fee, you can guess what it should be at first and alter it later as necessary.

Charging for Handling

When the fee you charge for shipping exceeds your actual carrier charge, the difference is considered to be a handling fee. If you'd like, you can also charge a separate, flat handling fee to cover the cost of shipping-related labor. But if you do, make sure it's reasonable. Excessive handling fees are usually prohibited by sales venues—and, to some extent, by law. Many crafters avoid this issue by treating labor and packaging materials as overhead expenses.

Accepting Returns

Accepting returns can encourage more sales and lower your risk of credit card or payment processor chargebacks. To establish a return policy, first decide on a reasonable time frame for accepting returns after customers place their orders. Common examples are one week or one month. Then consider whether other conditions apply. For example, do you accept returns only for items that are inaccurately described or defective, or can any item be returned with "no questions asked"? A good compromise is to accept all returns—but only within a very limited time frame.

Receiving and Processing Returns

You must also decide how to receive returns. When you sell online, customers can mail items back to you. When you sell in person, you can require that returns be mailed or allow customers to drop them off in person.

Term Tag

A restocking fee, which can be a set amount or a percentage of the purchase price, helps cover the cost of labor involved in processing returns. Charging one can also discourage frivolous returns.

You can offer customers either a refund or an exchange or a choice between the two. For refunds, determine which costs you'll reimburse, such as the full purchase price, the purchase price less shipping, or the purchase price less a *restocking fee*.

Possible Return Exclusions

You can have a different return policy for custom designs, which may be difficult to resell because you make them to a single customer's specifications. You might refuse returns of custom orders altogether, charge them a higher restocking fee, or accept them only for exchanges. Alternatively, you can consider custom returns on a case-by-case basis.

Be aware that health laws may prohibit the resale of certain goods, such as hats, headbands, earrings, and other body jewelry. Research the health laws in your town or city, state, and country to find out whether these rules apply. If so, you may want to exclude those items from your return policy.

Making a Quality Guarantee

With a quality guarantee, you promise to repair or replace an item if it proves to be defective within a set period of time. This policy is attractive to customers, but it increases the risk that those who improperly care for their purchases will pressure you to repair them for free.

Negotiating with Customers

As a practice, will you consider customer offers that are below your asking price? (If so, remember to mark up your prices to make room for haggling.) If not, be prepared to refuse low offers in a courteous, professional manner. Never assume that the haggler is trying to offend you with his or her request.

Also be prepared for times when customers ask for more than your policies and practices actually provide. Although it's important to try to accommodate every customer, don't be afraid to set limits on how much time or money you'll spend to do so. And when you need to refuse a customer, simply explain your situation calmly, courteously, and professionally.

Creating Alternate Policies

If you sell to resellers, you should establish separate wholesale policies. Some, such as payment terms, may be less restrictive while others—such as returns policies—may be more restrictive. We'll cover them in more detail in Chapter 18.

Also, some sales venues require you to have certain policies to protect customers, such as offering returns or guaranteeing safe delivery of shipments. If necessary, you can alter your policies to conform to these requirements on a per-venue basis.

The Least You Need to Know

- You should establish and maintain business policies and practices that govern how you operate as a seller.

- When you make policy decisions, weigh the risks and benefits of each possible approach and strive for a balance between encouraging more sales and protecting yourself.

- Write your policies for potential customers to read and consider.

- Know when a customer asks too much of you, and be prepared to courteously refuse unreasonable requests.

Chapter 8

Simple Promotion for the Casual Seller

In This Chapter

- ◆ Understanding the real value of your crafts
- ◆ Using word-of-mouth promotion
- ◆ Making the most of standard marketing materials
- ◆ Taking advantage of free promotion online and through your sales venue

Promotion—communicating with your target customers and introducing them to your crafts—is essential for selling. As a casual seller, you can keep it simple and affordable by employing some basic strategies for connecting with people. These include telling everyone you know about your craft, using business and information cards, sending out newsletters, and making the most of the Internet.

With this low-key approach to promotion, you don't need to buy advertising or aggressively market your wares. If you'd like to expand your approach later, you can try the strategies covered in

Chapter 15. After reading this chapter, see the Supplemental Appendix at www.craftychannels.com/resources for resources that can help you find the materials and services covered.

The Real Value of Your Crafts

In Chapter 5, we saw that in order to make a profit, you mark up your prices beyond what you need to cover your costs. You can make these markups because your crafts have greater value than the sum of their parts, labor, and assigned overhead expenses. That value is what you communicate to your target customers through promotion—what really motivates people to buy.

During the pricing process, you identify factors that add value to your goods, such as the rarity or uniqueness of components, trendiness (or antitrendiness), and positive media attention. These are the benefits you should focus on when you promote your crafts.

Spreading Your Own Rumors

The simplest way to promote your wares is by word of mouth: telling everyone you know about them. Often, just mentioning that you sell crafts sparks people's curiosity, and they'll want to know more. Some of those people will mention your crafts to other people. Some will even volunteer to pass out your business cards. In business-speak, this is called viral marketing. It initiates a chain of communication that gets your crafts noticed.

Word-of-mouth promotion can be casual and unintimidating, making it a great option if you're not comfortable in the role of a salesperson. But keep in mind that getting the initial word out is only the first step. From time to time, you need to remind potential customers about your crafts to keep them interested.

Business Cards

Handing out business cards is an easy way to start establishing yourself as a seller. You can also leave them in small stacks at local businesses (with permission) and include them with packaged orders. Each card should include, at a minimum, your seller name, a brief description of what you sell, your phone number, and your e-mail address. Optionally, you can include your mailing address and the URL of any websites you use for selling or promotion.

Bits and Pieces

Use a word-processing program to create a letterhead when communicating with people in writing. A letterhead is printed at the top of sheets of paper and includes your seller name, contact information, and optionally a graphic design. It should match the color scheme and overall style of your other marketing materials.

Ordering Business Cards

Some online printing companies sell very affordable custom business cards. You can use premade designs that you amend and enhance with your own text and colors or make your own designs using photographs of your work or graphics that you create from scratch. It's usually free to experiment with card designs on these sites, and you're charged if you place an order for printing. Although some sites purport to offer free business cards, be sure to read the fine print before accepting those offers. At a minimum, they usually require that your cards include advertising for the printing company.

Another option is to order custom business cards from an independent graphic artist. A good way to find one is to search shopping websites, such as Etsy.com, using the term "business cards."

Making Business Cards

If you have the time and necessary skills, you may be able to save money by making your own business cards. A common approach is to use a business card template included with your word-processing program. You can design cards and enter text, then print them on card-stock or precut, printable business cards from an office supply store. Be aware, however, that these cards rarely look as nice as professionally printed cards.

Information Cards

Information cards are larger cards that tell customers about you and your work. They are especially useful when you sell in person. You can keep a stack on hand to give out or scatter a few throughout your display area. If possible, design them to match your business cards in overall style.

Types of Information Cards

At a minimum, you should have an "About the Artist" information card that includes your name, the city or town where you live and craft, a general description of your craft medium, and the benefits that give your goods extra value. Place at least one copy in your display area, either lying flat, propped up, or in a picture frame.

You can also use information cards that:

◆ Describe each category of your goods

◆ Explain your crafting process

◆ List your policies

◆ Identify the raw materials you use

◆ Provide a schedule of future sales events that you plan on attending

Making Information Cards

Although you can order customized information cards from the same online printers that sell business cards, it's usually more convenient to make them yourself. You probably won't need as many information cards as you do business cards, and you'll benefit from having the ability to edit and print them whenever you'd like.

You can use a word-processing program and print your cards onto full sheets of cardstock or onto precut, printable cards from an office supply store. Typical sizes are a full 8½ by 11–inch sheet or a half sheet, but you can find quarter sheets and foldover cards as well. Be sure to use your marketing colors and a font that accurately expresses your style.

Bits and Pieces

Consider using color photos on some of your information cards to catch customers' attention. For extra impact, print them separately onto photo paper and glue them onto your cards. You can even embellish them with scrapbooking borders or backgrounds.

Newsletters

Newsletters are informal publications that you regularly send to a list of subscribers. You can use them to announce new designs, venue changes, and sales events, but they're most effective when they also contain general information that your target customers will find useful.

Writing Newsletters

You can create your newsletters using a word processor and newsletter template and print them onto colored paper for mailing and handing out. Keep them relatively brief (not more than about two pages), date each issue, and include at least five basic sections:

1. Table of contents or "In This Issue" section

2. Greeting or introduction

3. Updates and announcements

4. An interesting or helpful article

5. Closing paragraph

The interesting or helpful article is what makes your newsletter especially valuable to readers. Use it to tell a story about your crafting life, describe a technique or raw material, give advice about buying gifts, or even share your knowledge about cooking, decorating, pets, parenting, or traveling. Your closing paragraph can tip readers to what they'll find in the next issue or simply remind them how to contact you with questions.

Digital Newsletters

Instead of printing and mailing your newsletters, you can send them by e-mail. If you sell online, you can even link them directly to your sales venue. However, you need to be very careful to avoid having your e-mails flagged as spam—and ultimately blocked—by Internet service providers. First and foremost, avoid sending your newsletter to anyone who didn't voluntarily sign up to receive it. Next, limit the number of recipients that you include in the "To:" field of a given e-mail; some spam filters block e-mails that are sent to groups.

Of course, limiting recipients can make it difficult to e-mail people on a list. A good solution is to sign up with an e-mail marketing service that sends your newsletters for you in a way that keeps them from getting flagged. Some services provide easy-to-use newsletter templates as well as statistics about how many people read your newsletter. If you go this route, first find a service that's affordable, then do some research to make sure it has a good reputation among craft sellers. The Supplemental Appendix at www.craftychannels.com/resources lists some possibilities.

> **Hitting a Snag**
>
> Don't send printed or digital newsletters so often that they annoy subscribers—nor so rarely that they forget who you are by the time one arrives. Try scheduling them biweekly, bimonthly, or somewhere in between.

Newsletter Subscription Lists

You need a newsletter subscription list to record the names and contact information of people who want to receive your newsletters. When you sell in person, always keep a sign-up sheet or stack of sign-up forms—along with a pen or pencil—in your display area. If you sell online through a shopping site, check to see whether it offers an e-mail sign-up function. If it doesn't, consider asking customers who place orders for permission to add them to your own list.

To protect your reputation and comply with antispam laws, never share your subscriber list, and certainly don't sell it. Make it clear to subscribers that you protect their privacy by adhering to this rule.

Craft Blogging

If your target customers spend time on the Internet, you can find lots of ways to reach out to them for free. One of the best tactics is to create and maintain a blog. You can use a traditional blog, such as one provided by WordPress or Blogger, and/or a microblog, such as Twitter.

Traditional Blogging

When you sign up with a free blogging service, you receive an easy-to-use website where you can post updates, tell interesting stories, and share photos of your latest creations. You might even choose to share personal information and updates about your life to help potential customers get to know you.

Start your blog using a template provided by the blogging service, and customize it as best you can to match your marketing colors and style. But don't get too wrapped up in design; especially as a casual seller, your most valuable blog assets are content and consistency. Get creative with your posts to keep readers interested, and write a new post at least once per week.

Microblogging

With microblogging sites, you can post short snippets of text whenever you choose. Using one correctly can help you find customers; the trick is to write posts that are not obvious advertisements but contain words that your target customers are likely to search for. Here are some ideas:

- Announce your latest regular blog post and link to it.

- Announce the publication of your most recent newsletter and link to subscription information.

- Comment on and link to articles or blog posts that interest your target customers.

- Describe your raw materials purchases and design ideas.

- Occasionally mention and link to new listings on your online sales venue.

Microblogging services are similar to e-mail lists in that you need to avoid breaking antispam rules. Read through the service's terms and conditions before you get started to find out what you can and can't do. If you also keep a regular blog, be sure to add a link there inviting people to follow your microblogging posts.

Social Networking

Social networking sites, such as Facebook, bundle together lots of online tools that you can use to promote your crafts. As long as you follow the rules, you can use these sites to post announcements, photos of new designs, and dates and locations of upcoming sales events. They're also a good way to communicate with and receive feedback from potential customers.

Bits and Pieces

Some payment processors provide code that you can paste into your blog or social networking site page to list your crafts for sale. You'll begin learning about selling on the Internet in Chapter 9.

Recall that there are two general types of social networking sites: general-interest sites for everyone to use and topical sites for people with specific interests. If you use a general site, try to join interest groups that expose you to people most likely to be interested in your crafts.

After you set up a page on a social networking site, search for users that fit your target customer profile and invite them to join your friends or followers list. You can entice them by adding a gallery to your page with eye-catching photos of your best work. Many sites also allow you to link directly to your online sales venue.

As with blogging, it's important to update your social networking site regularly. You should also make every effort to comply with the site's terms and conditions governing commercial or business use.

Online Forums

In online forums, visitors create posts called "topics" in which they ask questions or make general comments. Other visitors can then reply to those topics. Forums can be extremely useful for researching and finding information—and, to some extent, you can also use them for promotion. To find forums, search online using key phrases that your target customers are likely to use.

Forums typically have strict rules controlling their use. Most prohibit solicitations of any kind, and some even limit the kinds of sites you can link to within a post. It's essential that you learn and follow these rules to avoid getting banned and tarnishing your reputation.

The most acceptable way to use forums for promotion is to join in as a real participant, offering advice and having honest conversations with other members. You can then include a signature at the bottom of your posts that contains your seller name—and, if allowed, a link to your blog or online sales venue. When forum readers want to learn more about you, they can click your link.

Be selective about the forums you use for promotion. They should be places where your target customers spend time—not just places where other crafters hang out. (Although you can make sales to other crafters, your target market probably extends well beyond them.)

Sales Venue Promotion

Sales venues offer their own promotional opportunities for sellers. In-person venues such as craft shows may list your seller name and contact information in brochures and on websites, and they typically allow you to use signs and banners. Online shopping sites include your listings in search databases, and they may occasionally feature your crafts in galleries on the home page. Although you can use these services to your advantage, I don't recommend relying on them as your sole means of promotion. You can usually make more sales by reaching out beyond your sales venue.

The Least You Need to Know

◆ When you promote your crafts, focus on the special benefits that give them extra value.

◆ Simple word of mouth can be an easy and effective means of promotion.

◆ You can also make use of business cards, information cards, and newsletters to communicate with potential customers affordably.

◆ Blogs, social networking sites, and forums can be valuable places to promote for free online as long as you follow their rules.

Part 3

Sales Venues for the Casual Seller and Beyond

Here's where you finally get to start selling. Many crafters begin with an online shopping site such as Etsy or ArtFire, so that's where we'll start. Next, we'll talk about auction sites (such as eBay) and how you might use them. We'll finish by exploring two great options for selling casually in person: trunk shows and sales parties. As you explore all of these venues, keep in mind that you can continue to use them if you decide to become a more serious seller.

Chapter 9

Online Shopping Sites

In This Chapter

- ◆ Understanding how shopping sites function
- ◆ More help selecting the right shopping site
- ◆ Getting started on a shopping site
- ◆ Listing items for sale and taking care of orders

Online shopping websites—such as Etsy (www.etsy.com), Artfire (www.artfire.com), and 1000 Markets (www.1000markets.com)—are popular for selling crafts because they're affordable, convenient to use from home, and expose your work to people all over the world. They're great venues for getting started, and you can continue to use them even if you become a serious business.

This chapter covers what you need to know about using any shopping site. When you select a particular site, be sure to read through its FAQs and seller terms to learn how to make the most of its unique functionality.

How Shopping Sites Work

Shopping sites function by collecting and storing information about the goods you have for sale, making that information available to online shoppers, and giving shoppers a way to make purchases.

Listings and Shops

Items for sale on shopping websites are usually called listings. Each shopping site is a database containing many listings created by numerous sellers. Every seller is assigned a website or a set of pages for showcasing their listings. These pages are typically called shops.

Your shop, which has its own URL, is where you direct customers when you promote your listings on other sites, such as your blog. It's also where you provide links to your written policies, biography, and contact information.

Categories and Searches

The two most common ways for shoppers to find your listings are by browsing categories and running searches. On most shopping sites, listings are organized into two types of categories: main categories and shop categories. You can assign both types of categories to your listings.

Main categories are created by the shopping site managers and typically appear on the site's home page. They often cover a broad range of crafts, such as Accessories, Candles, Clothing, Housewares, Jewelry, and Knitting.

Shop categories are created by sellers and appear only in shops. You can make them broad or specific, and you're usually free to name them whatever you'd like. For example, if you crochet, your shop categories might be "Scarves," "Hats," "Dishcloths," and "Wrist Warmers." Optionally, you might also create a category just for Sale items, to help customers locate them quickly.

There are also two types of searches: site (or main) searches and shop-level searches. Site searches scan listings across the entire shopping site, and shop-level searches scan for listings only within your shop. Soon after you create a listing (usually within about 24 hours), the listing becomes "indexed" so that it can be found in site searches. However, *where* it appears in searches—whether it's the first listing shown or the 800th—can be influenced by a number of factors, which we'll cover in the "Creating Listings" section later in this chapter. Alternatively, customers may find your listings by using an Internet search engine.

> **SOLD** | **Selling Secrets** _____
>
> Your shopping site controls which information in your listings is given priority by search engines. Read any information that your site provides about its search engine optimization (SEO) methods, and follow its advice for making your listings search engine friendly.

How Customers Place Orders

To place an order, a customer clicks a link to deposit an item into a virtual shopping cart. Within the cart, he or she can commit to the purchase by "checking out." This usually involves providing a shipping address, selecting a shipping method (when you offer choices), and entering payment information. However, as you may recall from Chapter 7, shopping website customers are not always required to pay right away. When they do not, you may need to send them a follow-up message or invoice.

Selecting a Shopping Site

In Chapter 2, I stressed the importance of selecting sales venues that match your style and attract your target customers. Now let's look at some other important factors.

Juried vs. Unjuried Sites

Some shopping sites are unjuried, which means that anyone can sign up and create listings. With juried sites, only approved sellers can create listings. A juried site may refuse your application if your goods, photos, product descriptions, policies, or marketing style fail to meet their standards.

There are pros and cons to using either type of site. Unjuried sites are easier to sign up with, and you can start selling right away. But with juried sites, your listings are less likely to appear beside low-quality or inappropriate listings in site search results, and you may have fewer listings to compete with overall.

Comparing Fees and Features

Most shopping websites charge one or more of the following types of fees:

- A one-time setup or sign-up fee
- Monthly or annual service fees
- Listing fees, charged each time you list an item
- Per-transaction fees, charged when you sell an item

Setup, service, and listing fees are typically fixed, whereas per-transaction fees may be fixed, a percentage of each sales transaction, or a combination of both. Listing fees usually cover a listing for a set period of time, called the listing duration, after which you need to relist and pay the fee again if your item hasn't sold.

Shopping sites differ on the exact services, or features, they provide. You should take both fees and features into account when comparing sites. One approach is to create a shopping site comparison sheet that includes fields for fees, listing durations, and notes.

In the following sample sheet, I compare two hypothetical shopping websites. The second site offers two payment plans to choose from, which I labeled "Plan A" and "Plan B." Neither site charges a setup fee, so I left that out.

This information is helpful only if I do a little work to apply it to my situation. Let's say I've decided that I won't list more than two new items each week. My goal is to make between about two and four sales per month, with an average sales price of $40. These are rough estimates, which is fine when I'm just starting. Here's how I might use them to compare shopping sites in a meaningful way.

Sample Shopping Site Comparison Sheet

Site Name	Monthly Fee	Annual Fee	Listing Fee	% Per-Transaction Fee	$ Per-Transaction Fee	Listing Duration	Notes/Special Features
ArtSee	None	None	$0.45	5%	None	4 months	Unjuried; guarantees featured seller status at least one day per month; mixed reviews
Crafters Unite–Plan A	$15.00	None	None	4%	$0.49	6 months	Juried; allows unlimited shop categories; more good reviews than bad
Crafters Unite–Plan B	None	$120.00	None	3%	None	6 months	(same as above)

Example of a shopping site comparison sheet.

First, I can estimate how much money I'll spend if I don't make any sales at all. This is money that I'm at risk of losing. Because ArtSee doesn't charge a monthly fee, my only nonsale related charges are listings fees. Crafters Unite doesn't charge listing fees, but it does have monthly and annual fees unrelated to sales.

Next, based on my estimated two to four sales per month, I can calculate my per-transaction fees for both sites. Combined with my monthly nonsale related charges, they represent my total monthly charges.

Here are my results:

Shopping Site Monthly Charge Comparisons

	ArtSee	Crafters Unite–Plan A	Crafters Unite–Plan B
Estimated monthly charges if no sales	$3.60	$15.00	$10.00 (paid in advance for one year)
Estimated monthly charges for two to four sales	$4.00–$8.00	$4.18–$8.36	$2.40–$4.80
Total monthly charges:	**$7.60–$11.60**	**$19.18–$23.36**	**$12.40–$14.80**

Comparison of estimated monthly charges for hypothetical shopping sites.

Now I can see that Crafters Unite Plan A is the most expensive option, so I'll probably cross it off the list. ArtSee has the lowest total monthly charges, whether or not I make sales, and it grants me a free promotional opportunity as a featured seller. However, its listing duration is shorter than Crafters Unite, and I found that it has mixed reviews among its users when I did some research.

Crafters Unite Plan B has pretty reasonable monthly charges plus a longer listing duration and better reviews, but it charges the equivalent of $10 per month even when I don't make a sale—and I must pay that fee in advance for an entire year. That convinces me that ArtSee is probably my least-risky option.

Shopping Website Terms and Conditions

Terms and conditions—sometimes called terms of use, user agreements, or site policies—are rules for what you can and can't do on a particular shopping site. Before you sign up with a site, read through its terms and conditions and make sure that you can comply with them. Here are some typical examples:

- You may only list items that you personally made by hand.

- You may only list items that you made by hand, commercial crafting supplies, or vintage items that are at least 20 years old.

- Your product descriptions must be accurate and not misleading.

- You may not use your shop or listings for the sole purpose of redirecting visitors to another website or sales venue.

- You may not use the site messaging system to send unsolicited advertising to other site members.

- Your business policies must not conflict with the shopping site's policies.

- You may not do anything to avoid paying fees, such as completing a transaction off site.

- Your shipping and handling fees must be reasonable.

Terms and conditions are usually accessible from a site's home page or through a link at the bottom of other pages. Take these rules seriously. If you violate them, the site may close your shop and delete your listings.

Getting Set Up

Your shopping website will walk you through the process of signing up and creating your shop for the first time. Here's a look at what's usually involved.

Registering a Username and Password

To sign up, or register, with a shopping site, you typically create a username and password. Your username becomes your identifier as a member of the site, and it's typically shown when you use the site forum or send messages to other members. It might also appear in your shop's URL. You can use your seller name as a username or select something that's easy to remember and descriptive of your craft and style. Choose wisely, because some sites prohibit you from changing your username later.

Writing a User Profile

Your user profile, or "bio," tells shoppers about you and your craft. I recommend making it at least one paragraph long but not more than three. Introduce yourself and your techniques, then describe the special benefits of your products. Optionally, you can tell a story about how you got started crafting, explain the inspiration behind your work, or describe media attention you've received. This is a valuable opportunity to connect with—and rope in—your target customers.

Entering Your Policies

Shopping sites also provide an area for entering your business policies. Oddly, not all sites require that you do this—but you should. Shoppers deserve to know what they're agreeing to if they buy from you, and your customer-friendly policies can encourage more sales.

You should have a set of written policies in place after reading Chapter 7. (If you don't, go back and do that now.) Take the time to compare them with your shopping site's policies, and make any necessary changes to conform them to those rules. Then simply insert them into your policy section.

Bits and Pieces

It's a good idea to use a word processor to write your profile, policies, and product descriptions. This allows you to run a spell check and copy and paste the text into the appropriate section on the shopping website. You'll also have a copy of your text if the site malfunctions and deletes your entry.

Setting Up Shipping Profiles

Most shopping sites allow you to set up shipping profiles for applying flat shipping fees to listings. You can create one profile for each shipping fee that you charge. For example, using my fee chart from Chapter 7, I might create a profile called "Tier 1 First Class" for my first weight category of packages. When I assign that profile to a listing, the shipping fee automatically becomes $2. With many shopping sites, you can also include multiple-item shipping fees in profiles. If I set mine at 50¢, the shipping fee in my listing would become "$2, or $0.50 if shipped with another item."

Uploading a Banner

Often, you can upload a long, narrow graphic to use as a shop banner. You can make your own using a computer graphics program such as Photoshop or PaintShop, or you can hire a graphic artist to customize one for you. Search your shopping site using "banner" or "custom banners" as search terms to find these services. Be sure to select a design that appeals to you and your target customers, because it's one of the first things shop visitors see.

Choosing Shop Categories

You should also focus on your target customers when creating your shop categories. What kinds of categories will be most useful for them? The simplest approach is to use general descriptions of the items you make, as in the example of crochet categories earlier in the chapter. Alternatively, you can use collection names, colors, or price ranges as categories.

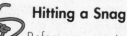

Hitting a Snag

Before you create shop categories, research whether your shopping site uses them as key words when submitting your shop to search engines. If so, don't get too creative with your category names; make them simple, descriptive words or phrases that your target customers are likely to use as Internet search terms.

Creating Listings

Once your profile, policies, shipping profiles, and banner are in place, you're typically ready to start creating listings.

Assigning Categories

One of your first tasks is to assign categories for your new listing. Normally, you can select one or more main categories and one or more shop categories from separate drop-down lists.

Devising a Title

You also need to give your listing a title. How you should word titles depends on how your shopping website uses them. If it treats titles as search terms, either on the site or through Internet search engines, then you should make them simple, clear, and descriptive. If your shopping site doesn't use them for searches, you can use design names or other stylized terms. For example, if my site uses titles for searches, I might use "Beaded Leaf Pendant Necklace" as a title; but if it doesn't, I could use "Mallorca Necklace" or even just "Mallorca."

Writing a Product Description

There's an art to writing effective product descriptions, and you'll get better at them over time. Start by browsing other listings on your shopping site for examples. It's usually best to keep descriptions relatively brief while still including all of the information shoppers need to make a purchase decision. That includes dimensions, materials, and colors (especially because colors can be inaccurate on computer monitors). But your descriptions don't need to be lifeless. Shoppers often appreciate descriptions with personality. Try mentioning what inspired you to craft the item, what you love most about it, or something interesting about the materials you used.

Taking and Uploading Photos

Photos are the most important elements of your listings; they're how online customers experience your crafts, and they set a tone for your listings that can add to or subtract from your goods' perceived value. Unfortunately, taking stylish, high-quality photos isn't easy. Some crafters spend months or even years struggling to achieve their desired results. If this happens to you, try not to get discouraged—it's just part of the process.

To take adequate photos, you'll need a good digital camera and a proper source of lighting. Your camera should have a macro function for closeup shots and a semi- or fully manual focus mode for maximum control.

Many crafters achieve their best results shooting outdoors on sunny days. If you shoot indoors, consider purchasing a set of tabletop photography lights and a light-filtering photo tent. Alternatively, you can save money by making your own photo tent. I've listed some resources for lights, tents, tent project instructions, and general digital photography information in the Supplemental Appendix at www.craftychannels.com/resources.

Even when you have a good camera and adequate lighting, you may need to touch up your photos using photo-editing software such as PaintShop or Photoshop. You must then save the photo files to your computer in the format required by your shopping website and follow the site's instructions for uploading them. Whenever possible, upload several photos of the item taken at different angles. Keep in mind that not every photo needs to show the entire object; some can be partial closeups.

Bits and Pieces

Check your shopping site's guidelines for suggested photo dimensions. If your photos are too small, they may appear stretched or blurry in the listing—and if they're too large, they may load slowly.

Entering Shipping and Payment Information

If you have shipping profiles (see the section "Setting Up Shipping Profiles" earlier in this chapter), select one for your listing. To decide which profile to use, you may need to weigh the item using a postage scale and estimate the weight of shipping materials it will require.

Most shopping sites allow you to select your accepted payment methods from a list or drop-down menu so that they appear in the listing. Check to see whether you can set default values for these based on your payment policies.

Adding Tags

Your shopping site might also allow you to enter descriptive key words, or "tags," to your listings. These are normally used for website searches; when a shopper searches for one of your tags, your listing is included somewhere in the search results. Your tags should honestly describe the item in your listing. For the Mallorca necklace, I might use the following tags: necklace, beaded, black, onyx, silver, leaf, pendant, women's, nature, boho, and Bohemian.

Some shopping sites permit you to use your seller name as a tag to help shoppers find you. But aside from your seller name, never use a tag that doesn't accurately describe the item in your listing. This is considered misleading and can result in your listing being canceled.

Checking Your Listing

Before you submit a listing, check it carefully for misspellings, inaccuracies, or photo problems. Once it's listed, review it again to make sure it looks and functions the way you intend. After a day or so, you can run site searches to find out where it appears in the results. Just remember that its search ranking will change over time as other sellers create new listings and older listings expire.

Getting Found in Site Searches

Earlier in this chapter, I mentioned that certain factors determine where your listings appear in site search results. Those factors, and their priority, differ from one shopping site to the next. On some sites, newer listings appear before older listings by default. Accordingly, the more often you create new listings, the more likely they'll be found in searches. On these sites, some sellers make a habit of canceling unsold listings before they expire in order to relist them sooner. This adds to the cost of selling online, but it can lead to more sales.

Other sites design their searches to bring up the most relevant listings based on tags, titles, and descriptions—regardless of when listings were created. Check your site's FAQs or search its forum posts for tips on making the most of its site search rules.

Monitoring Your Listings

Most shopping websites provide statistics that indicate how many times your shop and listings are viewed. If your views are low, try revising your titles and tags, retaking photographs, creating new listings on different days of the week or times of day, or increasing your promotion efforts.

Processing Sales

Processing a shopping site sale involves receiving cleared payment and shipping the order. A transaction is normally considered complete when you give and receive feedback.

Invoicing and Receiving Payment

You should receive an e-mail notification whenever a customer places an order through one of your listings. You can then log in to the shopping site to confirm whether the customer has paid. If not, you can send him or her an invoice using your online payment processor or a direct message thanking him or her for the order and noting the amount due.

Keep in mind that with most online payment processors, customers are not limited to using their credit cards. They may choose to pay by debiting their bank account (this is sometimes called an "e-check"). As with paper checks, these debits take some time to clear. Always confirm that an online payment has actually cleared before shipping an order.

Shipping Orders

Once you receive cleared payment, you can package the customer's order and ship it. Follow the shipping procedures you decided on when you established your policies and practices, and be sure to comply with any carrier shipping rules. For example, when you print a dated U.S. Postal Service postage label from the Internet, you must mail your package on that same day.

Keeping in Touch with Customers

Communication is key to establishing a good reputation as a seller and encouraging repeat orders. Although you should never send unsolicited e-mail or messages to potential customers, always respond to questions promptly. When a customer makes a purchase, update him or her on every change in the status of his or her order. Send a courteous e-mail or message when payment is received but uncleared, when payment clears (and the order is scheduled for shipment), and when the order ships. If you use a shipment tracking service, paste the tracking number into your final e-mail or message.

Working with Feedback

Most shopping sites have feedback systems where buyers and sellers can publicly rate their experiences. Feedback can be positive, neutral, or negative and may include written comments about the transaction. Most shopping site users take feedback very seriously, so handle feedback issues with care. When a transaction goes relatively smoothly—that is, payment was received more-or-less on time and there were no problems—I recommend leaving positive feedback.

If a customer places an order but never makes payment or otherwise violates your policies, you need to make a judgment call about feedback. Be aware that if you leave neutral or negative feedback before a customer leaves feedback for you, they may "retaliate" by leaving the same—or worse—feedback. You always have the option of leaving no feedback at all for a transaction that goes poorly.

Bits and Pieces _____

As a practice, some sellers withhold feedback until they receive feedback from the customer. I generally follow this practice myself. However, it can be controversial. If a customer is unhappy with an order, he or she might be afraid to inform you or request a return for fear that you'll leave negative feedback. This can damage your reputation and result in fewer repeat sales. Try to avoid it by sending a follow-up e-mail or message to any customer who doesn't leave feedback within about a week after you ship their order. Courteously ask whether they received the package and have any questions.

The Least You Need to Know

◆ Shopping sites are databases of listings, and you need to understand how they work in order to get your listings noticed.

◆ When comparing shopping sites, note whether they are juried or unjuried, assess their fees, and weigh their features.

◆ Creating a listing is a multi-step process, and the decisions you make during that process influence how easily your listings are found by online shoppers.

◆ Open communication by e-mail or messaging is essential for developing strong online customer relationships.

Chapter

Online Auction Sites

In This Chapter

◆ The unique challenges of auction websites

◆ Strategies for using auction sites effectively

◆ How to sell on an auction site

Auction and shopping sites are similar in functionality, but their target audiences are quite different. For that reason alone, you probably won't use an auction site as your primary sales venue. Auction sites can also expose you to nastier competition than you find on shopping sites, and you may find it harder to manage auction site expenses.

There are certain situations when you might find it helpful to use one, however. Let's explore those and then take a brief look at how auction sites work. Because this chapter focuses on the differences between auction sites and shopping sites, be sure to read it in conjunction with Chapter 9.

Auction Site Challenges for Crafters

As I've already hinted, auction sites aren't great venues for crafters. That's why shopping sites, such as Etsy, have lured so many crafters away from auction sites such as eBay. If you decide to use an auction site, you need to understand what you're up against. Here's a closer look at the people you'll encounter.

Understanding Auction Shoppers

Auction sites attract two types of shoppers. One looks for discounts, hoping to buy goods for less than they're actually worth. That probably doesn't describe your target customer.

The second type hopes to discover rare and unique items—and if they get a great deal on them, all the better. Although this customer might occasionally shop for crafts, he or she is most likely to scout for antiques and vintage collectibles.

That doesn't mean your target customers never shop on auction sites, but they may be more likely to turn to shopping sites when looking for quality handmade crafts.

Understanding Auction Competition

Your competition on auction sites is also much different from shopping sites. Auction sites are packed with listings for imported, mass-produced goods. Your listings may seem overpriced when they appear in search results alongside these cheaper items.

Potential Ways to Use Auction Sites

So why use auction sites at all? In the following sections, we'll discuss the two most valuable uses for crafters: promotion and liquidation.

Promotion

You can create low-priced auction listings with the hope of attracting new repeat customers. Your goal is to entice those customers to buy from you again through a different, more profitable venue. If you go this route, be sure to budget your auction expenses and monitor your success over time—just as you would for any promotional activity.

> **Hitting a Snag**
>
> Auction site terms and conditions typically prohibit links to other venues in listings. To encourage your auction customers to visit a different venue, link to one in your thank-you e-mail when you make a sale. Check whether your auction site's rules allow you to invite those customers to join your e-mail list.

Liquidation

You can also use auction sites to unload, or liquidate, goods that you've had trouble selling at other venues. These can be older designs that have fallen out of fashion or early pieces that you crafted before finding your true artistic voice. Rather than keeping them in storage forever, try listing these goods on an auction site at reduced prices. Even if you take a loss (by selling below cost), you can recoup some of your expenses while freeing up physical storage space for more current designs.

How Auction Sites Work

Auction sites generally function like shopping sites, with some important exceptions. Here's what they have, and don't have, in common.

Item Listings

Auction sites usually offer several different types of listings to choose from. Traditional auction listings—called "auction-style" listings on eBay—run for a relatively short period of time, typically about one week. During that time, shoppers can place bids equal to or above a minimum bid price. "Fixed price" or "Buy It Now" listings have static prices and may have longer listing durations than auction-style listings.

Listings can also be a combination of types. For example, an auction-style listing can have a buy-it-now price that is higher than its minimum bid. These listings often have higher fees than regular listings.

Shops and Categories

Most auction sites give you the option of creating a shop or store for a separate monthly fee. Your shop pages contain all your auction and fixed-price listings, which you can organize into shop categories. As with shopping sites, shop categories are a more personalized way to organize your listings than simply using main categories.

How Shoppers Make Purchases

Most auction sites have shopping carts that customers can use to pay for multiple listings at once. Third-party auction cart services are also available, but they can be pricey and are more commonly used by sellers who have lots of listings to manage.

As with shopping sites, auction customers are usually not required to make immediate payment. You often need to follow up with customers and request payment by e-mail.

Auction Site Fees

Auction sites typically charge the following types of fees:

- ◆ Insertion fees, which are charged when you create a listing
- ◆ Additional fees for upgrades, such as bold titles or subtitles in search results
- ◆ Fees for special services, such as photo hosting, which is discussed later in this chapter
- ◆ Final value fees, which are charged when an item sells

An insertion fee is usually a flat fee based on your minimum bid, or starting price. For example, an insertion fee might be 50¢ for a listing with a starting price of between $7 and $22.99 but $1 for a starting price between $23 and $44.99.

Fees for upgrades and special services are also flat fees, and final value fees are normally a percentage of the sales price. Be aware that fee levels may differ from one listing type to another, and you may be charged extra for using more than one main category or selecting a longer listing duration.

Auction Site Terms and Conditions

Although auction site terms and conditions are often similar to those you see on shopping sites, keep an eye out for terms that are even more restrictive. For instance, you might not be allowed to charge a separate fee for shipping insurance.

Getting Set Up

You can sign up for a basic auction site membership by creating a username and password. This allows you to shop on the site; but in order to create listings, you must also register as a seller. You may need to submit credit card or bank account information, indicate how you'll pay your auction site fees, and disclose which payment methods you plan to accept from auction customers.

When your seller registration is approved, you can create a user profile (or "about me" page) and enter your policies, just as you would on a shopping site.

Creating Listings

When you create a listing on an auction site, you typically have more choices regarding duration, asking price, design, and shipping charges than you do on shopping sites.

Listing Durations

With an auction-style listing, you can select among short, medium, and long listing durations. Short listing durations (less than one week) usually have the lowest insertion fees. They can create a sense of urgency that motivates shoppers to place early bids, but they may reach fewer shoppers because of the limited time they appear in site search results.

Medium listing durations, which are usually one week, are the default when you create a listing. They're short enough to create some sense of urgency but long enough to be viewed in search results by quite a few shoppers.

Longer duration listings can be missed by shoppers searching for deals on listings that are "ending soon." However, they can still be useful for promotion or for fixed-price listings that shoppers find by visiting your auction shop.

Listing Prices

How you set a listing price depends on the type of listing you make. With auction-style listings, you need to select a starting price and decide whether to have a *reserve price*. Generally, lower starting prices attract earlier bids than higher starting prices.

> **Term Tag**
>
> A **reserve price** is the minimum price that you agree to sell an item for. Typically, you keep the reserve price private in hopes of encouraging bids. If the listing ends with bids that fall short of the reserve price, you have the option of selling to the highest bidder—but you are not obligated to, as you would be with nonreserve price listings.

For fixed-price or buy-it-now listings, you set a regular sales price just as you would on a shopping site. Some auction sites give you the option of accepting lower (or "best") offers on these listings for an extra fee.

The Effects of Auction Sniping

Bidding dynamics can be affected by the ability of shoppers to "snipe" auction-style listings. To snipe means to strategically place a bid in the final seconds before a listing ends. This can be done manually or with special software. Sniping can result in lower sales prices by effectively reducing competition among bidders.

For example, let's say there are several shoppers interested in your item, but they all wait to submit bids during the final two seconds before the listing ends. The winning bid will be the last bid received before the listing expires, which might be less than another bidder was willing to pay; a higher bid may have been received a fraction of a second too late. Moreover, early bids on auction listings tend to attract attention and encourage more bids. If all bidders "hold out" until the listing is about to expire, you miss out on this potential benefit.

Check your auction site's terms and conditions to find out whether they allow sniping, and if so, take this into consideration when setting your auction prices. (The popular website Ebay.com did allow sniping at the time this book was written.)

Uploading Photos

Unlike most shopping sites, auction sites don't normally allow you to upload multiple photos without paying an additional fee, called a photo hosting fee. However, you can upload photos to a different website and configure your listings to display them. This is called photo self-hosting. You can find free self-hosting services online or through your Internet service provider. Always check the terms and conditions of these services to make sure they allow commercial use.

Using Calculated Shipping Options

On some auction sites, you can choose to use calculated shipping in your listings, rather than charging a flat shipping fee. With calculated shipping, each customer's fee is automatically calculated when they check out, based on the weight information and carrier options that you entered when you created the listing.

You may find this helpful if you sell items with varying weights to a wide range of locations. But be aware that it's not foolproof. Customers can be overcharged or undercharged when you use calculated shipping, especially when they pay for more than one item at a time.

Preparing for Bids on Multiple Listings

When you have multiple auction-style listings running concurrently, you may sometimes have a situation where a customer bids—or plans to bid—on more than one listing at a time. When those listings end on different days, the customer usually prefers to delay payment for his or her first win until the other listings also end. This allows the customer to save on shipping by having all items shipped together.

Bits and Pieces

With online auctions, it's a good idea to paste your policies into each of your listings, even if you also link to them on a separate page. You can include them in a template, but be sure to edit them if your policies change.

To protect yourself from unending delays in payment, you should add a term to your auction policies that limits the number of listings that qualify for combined shipping. For example, you might state that only auctions that end within a period of seven days can be paid for together.

Designing Listings

You may have more control over the appearance of your listings on auction sites than you do on shopping sites. You can customize them with colors, extra photos, and graphics by coding them yourself or using an auction listing template. You can purchase a template premade or hire a graphic designer to create one for you.

Getting Found in Site Searches

Do some research to find out how your auction site prioritizes listings in site searches. Listing time, duration, and type can all be factors. For instance, a default site search may only bring up auction listings and not fixed-price listings from your shop.

Processing Auction Sales

You can process auction sales essentially the same way you process shopping site orders. Here's a look at what's generally involved.

Invoicing and Receiving Payment

After an auction listing ends successfully (that is, with a highest bidder or buyer), the customer is automatically notified by e-mail and reminded that payment is due. You can also send your own e-mail or onsite message thanking the customer for his or her purchase and providing payment instructions.

The closed auction listing typically contains a link that customers can use to check out, and you can also send them a direct link to your payment processor. Confirm whether a customer has made payment by signing in to the auction site and checking the status of the listing.

Keeping in Touch with Customers

It's a good idea to notify your auction customers about every change in the status of their orders, just as you would with shopping site customers. You can either send them e-mails or message them directly through the auction site. Also be sure to update the status of each order in the sold listings area of your auction site account.

Dealing with Nonpayment

Nonpaying customers may be more common on auction sites than on shopping sites. If a customer fails to make payment within a certain period of time, you typically can request a refund of some or all of your auction fees. Check with your auction site for its refund policies and deadlines.

Hitting a Snag

Unfortunately, auction sites are notorious for feedback squabbles. If you receive negative feedback in retaliation for reporting nonpayment, try to take it in stride. Rather than participating in an argument with the customer, stay calm and professional and continue doing your best to be fair in your dealings with customers. It won't be long before the negative comments get lost among the many positives you're bound to receive.

Monitoring Your Progress

Because auction site fees can be higher and more variable than shopping site fees, you should keep careful track of your auction spending. Most auction sites provide sales reports that you access by signing in to your account. Print them out or download them to your computer, and periodically review them to make sure you cover your costs.

The Least You Need to Know

◆ An auction site may be a poor venue for making a profit on your crafts, but you still might decide to use one for promotion or liquidation.

◆ Before you start using an auction site, take the time to understand how it differs from a shopping site that caters to crafters.

◆ Track your progress on auction sites, and be especially careful not to overspend on fees.

Chapter 11

Trunk Shows and Sales Parties

In This Chapter

◆ How trunk shows work

◆ Potential show locations and sponsors

◆ What to do before, during, and after a show

◆ How sales parties differ from trunk shows

Trunk shows and sales parties are small, independent sales events that you organize yourself. They're a good way to get started selling in person and prepare yourself for the larger craft shows that you may want to pursue later (see Chapter 17).

Trunk Show Basics

Trunk shows were traditionally held by high-fashion clothing designers who carted their wares to boutiques in storage trunks. They would open those trunks to display their latest designs and accept wholesale or retail orders during the show. Today, crafters have embraced the trunk show as an effective way to sell in person.

Trunk Show Pros and Cons

Unlike craft shows, you rarely need to pay an up-front fee for a trunk show. Instead, you share sale proceeds with the owner of the venue. You also don't need to spend an entire day working a trunk show; most last between one and four hours. These benefits make trunk shows great for casual sellers who don't have much money or time to spare.

The tradeoff is that it takes some effort to plan a trunk show. You first must find a business owner willing to sponsor your show. Then you need to work with that sponsor to hammer out all the terms and details. When that's finished, you need to promote the show or help your sponsor promote it for you.

Where to Hold a Trunk Show

You may already know some business owners who'd be interested in sponsoring your trunk show. Where do you normally spend time outside home? Which of those places might best attract your target customers? In addition to retail shops, consider places such as these:

◆ Restaurants, cafés, and coffee shops

◆ Salons and spas

◆ Yoga, dance, and fitness studios

◆ Building lobbies

◆ Office conference rooms

◆ Music venues

Keep in mind that trunk shows are mutually beneficial for you and your sponsor, because the sponsor receives a cut of your sales and the show helps attract customers and positive media attention. Point out these benefits when you approach potential sponsors.

Approaching Sponsors

Introduce yourself to potential trunk show sponsors and explain that you're looking for a trunk show venue. This is easiest when the business owner or employees already recognize you. In other situations, you may feel more comfortable contacting the business owner, building manager, or office manager first by mail or e-mail. Send them a brief letter or message of introduction along with some photos of your crafts. Invite them to contact you to learn more about your idea.

Planning a Trunk Show

Your trunk shows will receive the most attention if you treat each one as a special event. Think of them as opportunities for people to socialize as well as shop.

Selling Secrets

So how much inventory do you need for a trunk show? As a general rule, try to bring as much as will fit on your table without looking disorganized or cluttered. Because you pay a fee only when you sell something, exactly how much inventory you bring is not as crucial as it is when you sell at an organized craft show that charges a flat booth fee.

Public vs. Private Trunk Shows

Most trunk shows held by crafters are open to the public: anyone can attend, regardless of how they hear about the show. With private shows, only attendees who receive personalized invitations may attend. You can hold a public show just about any time of the day or night, but private shows are typically held outside the sponsor's regular business hours. Public shows can last up to five or six hours, while private shows typically run from one to three hours.

Setting a Mood and Enticing Guests

You can encourage guests to spend time at your show by providing free refreshments, such as light snacks and drinks. You can also offer free gifts or gift bags or hold a raffle with one of your finished goods as the prize.

Planning Your Display Area

Most crafters use a portable table as the foundation of their trunk show display. Look for a relatively lightweight, folding model that fits easily into your vehicle. You may be able to find one at a camping supply store or big-box retailer. If craft shows are in your future, select a durable table that you can use later in your booth. Purchase or make a fabric cover for your table, or drape it with a table cloth, runner, or even scarves.

Bits and Pieces

Design your trunk show display before scheduling your first show. Know its dimensions so you can tell sponsors how much space you need to set up.

You also need a chair, display props (risers, racks, or shelves), and marketing materials such as information cards and business cards. Experiment with your setup at home to find a configuration that works. Take some photographs of your display to show to prospective sponsors.

Promoting a Trunk Show

Even if your show is public, you can still use invitations to help promote it. Send them by regular mail or e-mail to friends, family, co-workers, past customers, and everyone on your mailing list. If you purchase advertising (see Chapter 15), try styling your ads as public invitations.

Your invitations should match your marketing color scheme and overall style (see Chapter 6). At a minimum, include the following information:

- Your seller name and e-mail address or phone number

- The date, time, and location of the show

- A general description of the goods you'll have available for purchase

- The payment methods you accept

- Any refreshments you or the sponsor will provide

- Any free gifts and who receives them (such as a raffle winner or the first five guests to arrive)

- Any special discounts available only at the show

Optionally, you can encourage invitees to bring along friends and family. An RSVP request can help you anticipate the total number of guests, especially for private shows. If you become a more active seller, you may choose to promote your shows more aggressively by sending out press releases or announcements to local media.

Your sponsor may also decide to include your show in their own promotional campaign, which they may need your assistance designing.

Negotiating Terms with Sponsors

Before agreeing to a show, you should sit down with the sponsor and discuss some important details. First, decide how to split proceeds. Sponsors typically ask for a commission of between 10 and 50 percent of a show's gross sales. Make sure that the split you agree to is enough to at least cover your costs (see Chapter 5). If a sponsor cannot lower their cut to a level that works for you, courteously decline their offer and look for a sponsor who offers friendlier terms.

In addition to setting a commission, you and your sponsor need to decide on the basics of scheduling and show format, including date and time, duration, and whether the show will be public or private. For a private show, find out whether the sponsor has a guest list, and if so, whether you should also invite your own guests.

Here are some more topics to cover:

How much inventory will you bring, and how much space will you need to display it? To help the sponsor know what to expect, explain how much inventory you plan to bring and its price range. Work out ahead of time where you'll set up your table, keeping in mind its physical dimensions.

Who will process payments? If the sponsor is a retailer with a cash register and merchant account, they might agree to process your customers' payments and reimburse you for your percentage of sales after the show. The sponsor may or may not ask for separate compensation to cover the costs of processing payments, such as merchant account fees.

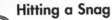

Hitting a Snag

If a sponsor processes payments for you, it doesn't mean that you're off the hook for those transactions when it comes to bookkeeping and inventory management. Ask your sponsor in advance to provide you with a list of sold items, along with how much each customer was charged, after the show. You may need to include product names or codes on your hang tags or labels to give the sponsor an easy way to identify them.

Who will provide refreshments? Decide whether you or your sponsor will supply food or drinks as well as napkins, plates, and cups or glasses.

How will your display be lighted? Find out whether the sponsor can accommodate your lighting needs. If not, plan to bring clip-on lights or lamps for your table. Check ahead of time for electrical outlets, and know whether you need extension cords.

Will you sit down or stand and mingle? To make a trunk show feel more like an art exhibit or party, you can stand up and mingle with guests rather than sit behind your table. However, this may be feasible only if the sponsor or their employees can help keep an eye on your display and process payments.

Who will pay for promotion? Occasionally, a sponsor requests extra compensation for their promotion efforts. Only agree to this if you think the terms are fair in light of the percentage split.

If you're dealing with your sponsor pretty casually, you can simply talk these details over. Or, you can put them in writing if you or the sponsor feels it's necessary. If a sponsor presents you with a premade contract, be sure to check it carefully for accuracy before signing.

Keep in mind that once you've done a few shows, you'll have some real sales data to share with potential sponsors—and, hopefully, more leverage to negotiate terms in your favor.

Before the Show

Make a list of everything you expect to take to the show (see the next section), and check off each item as you prepare. Keep everything carefully organized as you pack. Use labeled, stacking plastic storage boxes for finished goods and supplies.

A few days before the show, make a trial run at getting everything together and into your vehicle. Then take it out again and practice setting up, noting how much time the process takes. On the day of the show, plan to arrive at the sponsor's location at least that far in advance of the show's starting time.

What to Bring to a Show

We've already talked about bringing finished goods, a table and cover, chair, display props, and marketing materials to your show. Here are a few more things to think about.

Essential Supplies

Plan on bringing these items to every trunk show:

- Any bags, boxes, paper, or ribbons you'll use to package sold items
- A list of the finished goods that you bring to the sale (possibly in the form of your finished goods inventory list; see Chapter 4)
- Your mailing list sign-up sheet or forms
- A digital camera for taking photos of your display to use later for promotion
- Any lights that you need for your table
- If your goods are wearable, a tabletop mirror for customers to use when trying things on
- Any snacks, drinks, or raffle tickets that you plan to offer

- A calculator, receipt book, pen, clipboard, and *cash box* or *cash apron* with money for change

- Any equipment you need for processing credit cards, if you have a merchant account (see Chapter 12)

Term Tag

Most office supply stores sell **cash boxes,** which contain divided bins that keep paper money and coins separate and organized. **Cash aprons** (also called money aprons or vendor aprons) have sewn-in, fabric pockets for stashing cash, receipt books, and pens. They're less likely to be stolen than cash boxes but can be a little cumbersome to wear. Look for stylish, handmade versions on online shopping sites.

Money for Change

If you plan to accept payment yourself, visit a bank teller before the show to pick up small bills and coins for making change. You can withdraw money from your bank account or bring along larger bills to exchange.

You typically need between $50 and $200 in $10 bills, $5 bills, and coins for show change. How much you actually use depends on the number of sales you make and how you set prices. You can minimize the amount of change you need to give out by rounding prices to the nearest dollar and including sales tax in your prices (where allowed by state law).

Plan to keep your change money, along with the money that you receive from customers, in your cash box or apron. Be sure to write down how much money you bring for change so you can balance your books after the show.

Trunk Show Attire

You also need to decide what to wear to a show. Your clothing should be consistent with the style of your crafts but simple enough not to detract from your display. At the same time, avoid overly casual clothing unless it's consistent with the mood your sponsor sets for his or her venue. For fancier private shows, consider dressing as you would for a cocktail party.

Working a Trunk Show

Whether you sit behind your table or mingle with guests, do your best to relax and be sociable. Remember that most guests prefer a party atmosphere to a sales pitch, so don't get too aggressive about sales. Just be attentive and ready to answer questions about your crafts as guests browse them over.

When a customer asks to make a purchase, you can direct him or her to the sponsor's checkout area (if the sponsor is handling payment) or accept payment directly according to your payment policies. Use a calculator to carefully factor any tax and change, and record each charge and its payment method on both copies of the sales receipt (see Chapter 3).

If you have time during the show, you can also enter the sales information for each item sold on your finished goods inventory list. Otherwise, you'll need to do this later using your copies of the sales receipts.

What to Do After the Show

Your work isn't over when the trunk show ends. In addition to transporting your unsold inventory and supplies back home, you need to update your bookkeeping records, count your money, make sure that the inventory you brought to the show is accounted for, and—preferably—follow up with the sponsor and guests.

Updating Your Books

Before you unpack your inventory after the show, take the time to update your bookkeeping records. Go through your receipts (or the list of sales from your sponsor) and record each sale in your revenue journal, on each product inventory sheet, and—if you haven't already done so—on your finished goods inventory list. If you gave away any items as free gifts or prizes, be sure to record those as well. An option is to mark each as "sold" with a sales price of zero.

Total all the show's sales in your revenue journal, and set up a file folder for your show receipts. If the trunk show was one of your first, give some thought to how its sales might affect your tax status or any requirements for business licenses or permits that you don't yet have. (Refer to Chapter 13 for help.)

Counting Your Till

If you accepted payment directly from customers at the show, you also need to count your *till*. Then subtract that number from the amount of money you originally brought to the show for change.

> **Term Tag**
>
> Your **till** is the money that you keep in your cash box or apron. It includes both your change money and the cash and checks that you receive from customers.

The result should be the total that you received from sales. If it matches the total in your revenue journal (after updating it using receipts), you're good to go. But if it's different, you should try to determine why. A small discrepancy can result from giving a customer incorrect change, but a larger one might indicate a loss due to theft or a missing sales receipt.

If you cannot resolve a discrepancy, you should write it down for future reference. A simple approach is to record extra money (called an overage) in your revenue journal and missing money (called a shortage) in your expense journal. Doing so ensures that you can balance your books—and, when applicable, pay correct taxes.

After your till is counted and your books are up to date, deposit all your sales revenue into your bank account. This is necessary with personal checks but is also a good idea for cash because it makes it easier to reconcile your accounting reports and bank statements. However, avoid using an ATM machine to deposit cash; it's safer to hand cash to a bank teller who can give you a verifiable deposit receipt.

Finalizing Credit Card Transactions

At some point, you may choose to sign up for a merchant account so you can accept credit cards in person. Because those services typically require some financial commitment, we'll wait to cover them in Chapter 12. You'll see that the type of merchant account plan you have affects how much work you need to do after a show. For example, if your plan doesn't allow you to process credit cards in real time at a show, you'll need to process them at home—typically, over the Internet.

Checking Your Unsold Inventory

As you unpack your inventory, check each item against your finished goods inventory list to make sure that nothing is missing. If you can't find an item and have no evidence that it sold, or if you find something irreparably damaged, make a note of it on your finished goods inventory list. You may be able to expense the cost of missing or destroyed items, as well as any goods that you gave away, on your income tax return. (We'll talk more about deducting expenses in Chapter 13.)

Following Up with Sponsors and Guests

To make a good impression and help keep your crafts on people's minds, send personalized thank-you notes to your show sponsor and each guest who made a purchase. Thank the sponsor for their efforts, and if all went well, express interest in doing another show. Thank guests for their purchases and alert them to any future sales events that you've scheduled. Invite them to sign up for your mailing list if they haven't done so already.

Sales Parties

Sales parties are essentially trunk shows that you hold in your, or someone else's, home. They are private, invitation-only events with an even greater social focus than trunk shows.

The person whose home is used for a sales party is referred to as the host. You can be your own host or recruit a friend or acquaintance to host in exchange for something of value, such as a cut of the sales or a gift certificate for your crafts.

As with a trunk show, you should discuss the details of a sales party with your host ahead of time. The host is typically responsible for providing refreshments and inviting guests while the crafter accepts payment directly from customers.

When you set up for a party, you can use a dining table or other existing furniture for your display. Provide comfortable places for guests to sit and chat, and designate a spot for accepting payments. Use your cash box or apron and other essentials just as you would for a trunk show, and dress for a party. After the show, update your books, count your till, and check your unsold inventory.

Collaborative Trunk Shows and Parties

Although trunk shows and sales parties traditionally feature one seller, you can also collaborate with other crafters to hold larger sales. Look for local craft sellers with whom you share target customers and whose prices are similar to yours. Arrange to meet with collaborators before the show and work out all of the details and responsibilities, just as you would with a show sponsor or party host.

The Least You Need to Know

- Trunk shows are public or private sales events that you organize yourself with the help of a sponsor.

- You should plan out all of the details with your sponsor before agreeing to do a trunk show.

- Stay organized and keep track of your money and inventory before, during, and after a show.

- Sales parties are private trunk shows that you hold in your own home or in a host's home.

Part 4

Transitioning into a More Active Seller

If things go well and you decide to become more serious about craft selling, this is the part for you. We'll walk through the process of finding a business bank account, accepting credit cards with a merchant account, and doing some business planning. Then we'll look at what you can do to avoid legal trouble as a business, and I'll help you get ready to report the taxes that we first talked about in Part 1. Before moving on, we'll revisit the topic of promotion. You'll learn how you can get involved with advertising and track your promotional success.

Chapter 12

Becoming More Businesslike

In This Chapter

- Staying organized and becoming more professional
- Upgrading to business banking, bookkeeping, and accounting
- Getting smarter about online sales and shipping
- Using a merchant account to accept credit cards
- Business plans and business insurance

Preparing for more vigorous craft selling involves making some improvements and upgrades to your old systems and procedures. In this chapter, we'll look at where you can make changes that help you transition to the next phase of your venture.

Keeping a Calendar, Schedule, and Computer Backups

When you start selling more actively, time becomes a more significant factor in your decisions. To keep your life in balance, you should maintain a daily schedule and a calendar for tracking important dates, such as sales events and bookkeeping and tax deadlines. This will help you budget your time and set priorities. You can keep your calendar and daily schedule in a notebook or on your computer, or you can sign up for a free service such as Google Calendar.

It's also important to keep backups of your computer files, such as the data files for any bookkeeping and inventory management software you use (which we'll cover later in this chapter). You can manually make backup copies of files to store on portable memory storage devices or discs, or you can sign up for an online backup service that automatically makes backups for you. A good one to look into is Dropbox (www.dropbox.com).

Communicating as a Business

If you've been using your personal phone line and mailing address for selling, now is a good time to upgrade to a separate business line and address. You'll look more professional and better protect your privacy as your public exposure increases. Review Chapter 3 for some options.

Selling Secrets _____

> Although it's good to have a business phone and address, you probably don't need a fax machine. You can find other ways to send information electronically, such as using online forms and scanning and sending e-mail attachments. You can also send and receive faxes affordably at many office supply stores.

Business Bank Accounts and Credit Cards

Bookkeeping and budgeting tasks are easier if you keep your personal and business funds in separate accounts. You can usually sign up for a small business checking account at your local bank at little or no cost. Call your bank ahead of time to make an appointment with a banker and find out what you need to take with you. At a minimum, a copy of your business license, fictitious business name (if you have one), Social Security number, and personal identification are typically required. If you don't already have a business license, skip ahead to Chapter 13 and learn how to get one. Review Chapter 6 for information about fictitious business names.

When you open your business account, you'll have the opportunity to order business checks in either full-page sheets or single-check size. It's a good idea to opt for duplicate checks so you have a record of the date, amount, and recipient of every check you write. Keep in mind, however, that you're typically not required to purchase checks directly from your bank. You might save money by ordering them from a reputable online check printing service, or a membership retailer such as Costco.

Optionally, you can also apply for a business credit card, which can make it easier to track expenses—especially if you purchase supplies and services online. Banks sometimes sell "bundled" accounts, where a checking account, savings account, and credit card are provided together.

Business-Level Bookkeeping and Accounting

In Chapter 3, I explained how you can use simple expense and revenue journals for basic bookkeeping. When you become a more serious business, however, you need a more complete accounting system that helps you better analyze your progress and correctly account for expenses on your tax returns.

You have a few options here. First, you can hire a professional bookkeeper or accountant to manage your accounting system for you. Although this costs money, it frees up more of your time for crafting and selling, and it takes some weight off your shoulders at tax time.

Alternatively, you can purchase a small business accounting software program, such as Quickbooks, and maintain your accounting system yourself. If you go this route, expect a bit of a learning curve. You need to understand how your system works and how to use it properly to comply with tax laws. Accounting software also has its limitations. For example, as I'll explain later in the chapter, it usually fails to adequately track the costs of raw materials that become finished goods— something essential for deducting certain expenses on your tax returns.

A third option is to purchase accounting software and hire a bookkeeper or accountant to set it up and show you how to use it. You can then keep your own books throughout the tax year and submit a copy of your data, along with some additional information about your inventory, to an accountant at tax time.

Whichever method you choose, you or your bookkeeper or accountant will need some basic information to get started, including the value of the raw materials and finished goods that you have on hand. If you followed my recordkeeping advice in Chapters 3 and 4, you can glean what you need from your expense journal, revenue journal, raw materials inventory sheet, and finished goods inventory list.

Bits and Pieces

Don't throw away your old journals and other records after setting up a new accounting system. You may need them later to verify your starting balances. If you live in the United States, check the website www.irs.gov under "Businesses" and then "Small Business/Self-Employed" for guidelines on the length of time you should keep various records.

If you fell behind with recordkeeping as a casual seller, you should consult a bookkeeper or accountant for help—even if you plan to manage your accounting system by yourself going forward. You might be able to recreate past records by checking old receipts, counting inventory, or using careful estimates; but because everyone's situation is different and tax laws are involved, only one-on-one professional advice can ensure that you get started on the right foot.

Fine-Tuning Your Files

I've suggested using file folders to organize your receipts from vendors and copies of the sales receipts that you provide to customers. Once you're paying taxes as a business, you also need to keep records of any general expenses that might be deductible as business expenses.

These can be things such as the miles driven to and from in-person sales venues, money that you spend on food and drinks at craft shows, or fees that you pay to an accountant. Set up a file for each of these categories now (if you haven't done so already).

Using Online Sales Management Tools

If your online sales start to take off, look for software and online services that help you create listings and process orders more efficiently. Some of these have the ability to connect directly to a shopping or auction site so that you can use them to upload listings and download sales. Such services may be offered by third-party companies or by the venues themselves, sometimes for an additional fee.

Shipping More Orders

To speed up shipping, you can sign up for an online postage service such as Endicia or Stamps.com. These allow you to print prepaid postage labels in bulk using customer address data on your computer, and they also make it easier to buy private shipping insurance and ship internationally.

Optionally, you can use an electronic postage scale that plugs in to your computer and sends weight data to your postage service application. Thermal label printers also come in handy for printing labels quickly, and they don't even require ink. Check online auction sites such as eBay for deals on scales, printers, and labels that are compatible with your shipping service.

To make it easier to ship multiple packages on the same day, develop practices that help you avoid shipping a package to the wrong customer accidentally. For example, you might temporarily mark packages by hand with customer names and use sales receipts as checklists when you assemble orders.

Upgrading to a Merchant Account

In order to directly accept credit cards in person, you typically need to sign up for a merchant account. You can also use a merchant account to accept credit cards online without using a payment processor such as PayPal. Although you probably don't need a merchant account if you only sell online, you should have one if you plan to sell at craft shows and other large, in-person sales events where customers expect to pay with credit cards.

Selecting a Merchant Account

Large businesses use traditional merchant accounts, which are provided directly through banks. They have substantial monthly or annual fees, require a long-term commitment (often up to three years), and are complicated to manage from a bookkeeping perspective. If your bank offers you a merchant account application when you open your business checking account, it's a good idea to decline unless you've already researched—and ruled out—simpler and more affordable options.

I call those options "alternative" merchant accounts (see the Supplemental Appendix at www.craftychannels.com/resources for some examples). They are designed specifically for very small businesses, and you can sign up for one online. Typically, alternative merchant account providers offer a choice of plans with scaled fees that increase with the number and types of services you require. Fees may also be higher for lower-volume sales than for high-volume sales; however, monthly or annual service fees are usually reasonable.

In addition to monthly or annual fees, alternative merchant account providers charge a percentage of each sale that you process through them, plus a smaller flat fee for each transaction. The nice thing about these fees is that you pay them only when you make a sale.

Bits and Pieces

Some online payment processors now offer plans that function very much like merchant accounts. For instance, PayPal's "Virtual Terminal" allows you to process credit cards using the PayPal interface. (With standard PayPal, customers must sign in and enter their own payment information; you cannot enter it for them.) There are even Smartphone applications that provide access to Virtual Terminal. Because these pseudo merchant account plans have fee structures and application requirements that are similar to those of true merchant accounts, the tips in this chapter generally apply to them as well.

Signing Up

Signing up, or applying, for a merchant account usually involves submitting an online form with your name, business name, contact information, Social Security number or EIN (see Chapter 13), and some general information about your business, such as your sales volume, what you sell, and which sales channels you use. The merchant account provider uses this information to verify your identity and sometimes to perform a credit check before approving your application.

As part of the application process, you need to select a plan level. You can save money by enrolling only for the services that you really need. Be aware that merchant accounts often charge higher fees to process Discover and American Express cards than they do for VISA and MasterCard, so you may decide to select a plan that covers only VISA and MasterCard—at least, at first.

Accepting Credit Cards in Person

Once you have a merchant account, you can collect customer credit card numbers in person and submit them to your merchant account provider either online or over the phone. The method you use depends on your service plan and the resources you have available at the time and place of a sale.

Processing Charges in Real Time

If you have a phone or Internet access at your sales venue—and your merchant account plan allows it—you can process credit cards in real time (rather than later) in one of the following ways:

◆ Using an electronic card "swiper" provided by your merchant account provider for a fee

◆ Typing the credit card number into a secure, electronic form on your merchant account provider's website

◆ Swiping or typing the number into a secure Smartphone application provided by your provider

◆ Phoning your merchant account provider and reading the number to them

The main benefit of processing a credit card in real time is that you find out immediately whether a charge has cleared. It also eliminates the need to take card numbers home and process them later, leaving you responsible for protecting them from loss or theft.

Processing Charges Later

If you don't have access to a real-time processing method, or if your electronic method malfunctions, you may still be able to accept credit cards in person. Check with your merchant account provider first to make sure they allow this. At a minimum, your provider will probably require that you obtain an imprint of each card that you accept, rather than merely writing down its number.

To make imprints, you use a mechanical device called a card imprinter, or "knucklebuster," which stamps card information onto two copies of paper receipts called slips. You keep one slip copy to use when submitting the card number to your merchant account provider and give the other one to your customer. You can order a card imprinter and blank slips online or through some office supply stores.

Occasionally, a merchant account provider may require that you equip your imprinter with a merchant plate, which stamps your seller information onto each slip. You can also order a customized plate to give your customers more information about their purchases. It can include your seller name, contact information, and the name of your merchant account provider. (Your merchant account provider's name is especially useful when it, rather than your own business name, appears on customers' credit card statements.)

Practice using your card imprinter before taking it to a sales event. Remember that you need to write the total due on the top slip, obtain the imprint, and then have the customer sign the top slip before you separate the two copies. Keep your copy of each slip in your files for at least six months; you will need it if the customer initiates a chargeback, or payment reversal.

SOLD **Selling Secrets**

A federal privacy law in the United States prohibits customer receipts from including more than the last five digits of a credit card number or the card's expiration date. Unfortunately, most card imprinters print the entire card number and expiration date on slips. Some crafters address this by manually tearing, cutting, or blacking out that information on their customer's slips.

Accepting Credit Cards Online with a Merchant Account

In order to set up your merchant account to automatically process credit cards online, outside a shopping site or payment processor such as PayPal, you need an online credit card terminal called a payment gateway. Payment gateways are offered by some merchant account providers, but you can also subscribe to one through a separate company.

The easiest way to add a payment gateway to your own website is to sign up for a shopping cart service that connects to it. This typically requires you to register for the shopping cart and the payment gateway separately, then configure them to work together.

Another way to accept credit cards online is to use a service that collects card numbers so you can process them manually later. To protect your customers from potential identity theft, it's vitally important to use a service that *encrypts* information and stores it on a secure web server (see Chapter 16). Never ask a customer to send you a credit card number by e-mail or through an unsecured form on a website.

> **Term Tag** _____
>
> When data is **encrypted,** it's converted into an encoded, unreadable format. You can decipher the data by applying a secret piece of code called a key or by using software that applies the key automatically.

We'll cover shopping cart installation, payment gateways, and website security in more detail in Chapter 16.

Credit Card Security Rules

Don't take the responsibility of collecting credit card numbers lightly. You must follow specific rules and procedures both to comply with privacy laws and to earn customers' trust.

First, carefully read your merchant account provider's terms and conditions and perform all of the security measures that they encourage or require. These may include recording security codes from the backs of credit cards and obtaining customer addresses and signatures when you accept cards in person.

If you store credit card numbers on imprint-machine slips or on your computer, you need to take special precautions to protect them. Never throw old slips in the trash; always shred them completely. Keep unprocessed slips in your cash apron or locked in a secured cash box at sales venues. Make sure that you know where your slips are at all times, and don't allow anyone else to go through them.

To protect information on your computer, begin by installing firewall and antivirus software. It's also a good idea to encrypt files that contain sensitive information. Some operating systems, including Windows XP and Windows 7, have encryption applications built in. If you use third-party software to process credit cards, make sure it uses its own encryption.

Bits and Pieces

Privacy laws require you to store credit card numbers no longer than reasonably necessary for business purposes. That's usually the period of time within which your merchant account provider may honor a chargeback request. Set a schedule for yourself to permanently delete sensitive data on your computer, and shred old slips after that time elapses. For more information about protecting customer information, visit www.business.gov and www.onguardonline.gov.

Writing a Simple Business Plan

You should put together a simple business plan around the time you start selling with the goal of making a profit. It will help you put all the aspects of selling into perspective so you can make the best decisions for achieving your goals.

You can find lots of books and websites that offer business plan advice and provide examples to use as templates. I've listed some especially useful resources in the Supplemental Appendix at www.craftychannels. com/resources. Start by looking them over and getting a feel for how a typical business plan is structured, then take a stab at writing your own.

Keep in mind that most formal business plans are written for other people to read—typically, potential investors. Unless you're asking someone to invest money in your business, your plan can be simpler and more to the point.

At a minimum, it should include a "Financials" section with enough information and analysis to help you break even (cover your costs) and ideally make a profit. Your inventory and bookkeeping records should provide all the information you need to make the required initial estimates. Once you get going, your plan's financial reports will indicate whether and when you need to change your prices, reduce your costs, or make other changes.

Should You Buy Business Insurance?

Business insurance can provide some protection if you lose assets to theft, accident, or disaster or if your business becomes the target of a lawsuit. Whether you purchase insurance and how much coverage you buy depends on the degree of risk you're willing to assume.

Types of Insurance Plans

Different types of insurance plans cover different types of risks. One of the more worrisome risks for small businesses is liability, where someone sues you for causing harm to themselves or their property. Your liability risk may be higher than average if your finished goods are foods, children's items, soaps, cosmetics, candles, or are otherwise potentially hazardous.

Hitting a Snag

Don't expect your standard homeowner's, renter's, or automotive insurance policy to cover any business-related claims, even if you work from home and use your own vehicle for business purposes.

Another type of insurance, called business property insurance, covers the loss of or damage to your business's assets by events such as fire, flood, accident, or theft. This type of plan makes sense especially when you have a large inventory, pricey finished goods, or expensive tools and equipment.

It's also possible to buy policies that cover intellectual property claims (such as trademark infringement) or claims related to your e-commerce website. Don't forget that you also may need business-level automotive insurance for your vehicle.

Getting Coverage

Begin your quest for an insurance policy by finding out whether your current homeowner's, renter's, or automotive insurance can be amended to cover your business. If it can't be, or if an amended plan won't provide enough coverage, look for an agency that specializes in insurance for small businesses. Talk to a few local representatives, tell them about your business and the risks you want covered, and request quotes for varying levels of coverage. Most crafters are able to find an affordable policy this way.

While standard insurance policies provide a year's worth of coverage, it sometimes makes financial sense to purchase a short-term policy to cover a specific event. For example, some insurance agencies provide liability insurance for a single craft show.

Craft show organizers also sometimes invite vendors to buy into a group liability insurance policy for a show, but you should make sure you're comfortable with the coverage it provides before signing up.

The Least You Need to Know

◆ Bookkeeping, accounting, and budgeting are much simpler if you keep your personal and business finances in separate bank accounts.

◆ To comply with tax laws and properly manage your business, you should upgrade to a business-level bookkeeping and accounting system.

◆ If you sell at larger in-person venues, it's important to accept credit cards. Sign up for an affordable merchant account, and learn how to process cards correctly.

◆ Use a business plan to keep your business afloat and going in the right direction. It doesn't need to be as formal or detailed as the plans used by many large businesses.

◆ To better protect yourself from loss and liability, purchase business insurance.

Chapter 13

Staying Legal

In This Chapter

- ◆ A closer look at business licenses and permits
- ◆ Understanding—and tackling—your tax obligations
- ◆ Complying with craft-specific regulations

Now that you're getting more serious about selling, you need to be extra careful about complying with business laws and regulations. In this chapter, I'll explain how you can do just that. You'll see that legal requirements really aren't that frightening as long as you stay organized and commit to keeping up to date with the rules that apply to your business.

Getting Your Licenses and Permits

Licenses and permits grant you governmental permission to operate as a business. Some, such as business licenses, essentially serve as taxes. Others help protect people in the community from potential harm.

Although you may not need certain licenses and permits when you sell only occasionally, you'll likely need some as a more active seller. To find out which ones, check with your local chamber of commerce or your local or state agency that regulates businesses or collects taxes. This may be the revenue department, finance department, secretary of state, or franchise tax board.

Now let's take a more detailed look at the licenses and permits you might need.

Bits and Pieces

Don't forget that in addition to obtaining the necessary business licenses and permits, you may need to file a fictitious business name. Review the "What's in a Name?" section in Chapter 6 for details.

General Business License

A general business license allows you to do business in exchange for paying a recurring fee or tax. The fee is typically due annually and may be based on your level of revenue for the year. Although most business permits are issued locally, some U.S. states require you to apply for a state-level business license. One example is Washington State, where you must apply for a master business license. Whether you also need a local business license depends on the laws of your city or county.

Home Business Permit

A home business (or "home occupancy") permit allows you to work from home. In order to qualify, you must agree to comply with specific home-business rules that vary by jurisdiction. Among other things, these may limit the number of deliveries that you receive each week, the signs you can place on your property, the number of business-related visitors you receive, and the types and amounts of chemicals you store.

Permanent Seller's Permit

Seller's (or "resale") permits are usually issued at the state level and in many states give you permission to operate as a retail seller in exchange for collecting and remitting sales tax. You usually need a seller's permit for each jurisdiction within which you sell in person. Your "permanent" seller's permit is the one that you hold on an ongoing basis for the jurisdiction where you do most of your selling.

How much sales tax you owe, and when you need to collect and pay it, differs from place to place. Carefully read the information that arrives with your seller's permit, and be sure to follow all of your state's sales tax requirements. For example, some states require you to charge your customers separately for sales tax, while others allow you to include sales tax in your prices.

SOLD | **Selling Secrets** _____

A 1992 Supreme Court decision established that online sellers are not required to collect (or remit) sales tax in the United States on orders shipped to any state where they do not have a physical presence, such as an office or warehouse. However, various proposals to alter or reinterpret that rule were being presented to Congress around the time this book was written. Check for any changes in your state's sales tax rules, including this one, at least once per year.

In many states, your seller's permit also allows you to purchase raw materials without paying sales tax. To take advantage of this, ask your suppliers whether they offer tax-exempt sales to businesses. Typically, you'll need to provide the supplier with a copy of your seller's permit or its number, and you may be asked to sign a form called a resale certificate, in which you certify your intent to use the materials in goods that you sell at retail.

Temporary Seller's Permits

If you occasionally sell in person in a state not covered by your permanent seller's permit, you may need to apply for a temporary seller's permit. Many states grant these free of charge. Keep in mind that you need to file a separate sales tax return for each jurisdiction that grants you a seller's permit and comply with each state's sales tax rules.

Special Licenses

Certain types of businesses are required to have special local, state, or federal licenses. When it comes to crafts, these are usually aimed at enforcing health and safety regulations. They most often apply to food, cosmetics, soap, and (occasionally) clothing.

Hitting a Snag

Some special licenses impose significant restrictions on how and where you make your crafts. For instance, in some jurisdictions, you can legally produce food items only in a certified, commercial kitchen. If this sort of regulation applies to you, look for reasonable ways to comply, such as renting shared commercial kitchen space. It will increase your overhead expenses but also protect you from potentially large fines.

A good way to start researching these licenses is to ask other local craft sellers about them. However, never take what you hear by word of mouth at face value; always do your own follow-up research with the appropriate government agencies.

Filing Tax Returns

With your improved accounting system up and running (see Chapter 12) and your licenses in hand, you'll be set to start filing taxes as a business. Each category of taxes that you're responsible for has its own schedule that dictates when those taxes are due. Be sure to add each due date to your calendar, and always give yourself or your accountant enough time to prepare your tax returns in advance.

Here's a general look at the reporting requirements for each tax category.

Income Tax

As I pointed out in Chapter 2, you must report craft sales on your federal and state income tax returns. This rule applies whether you are a casual or more active seller and whether or not you make a profit. However, how you file depends on whether your venture qualifies as a hobby or a business. For example, in the United States, you report sales from a hobby as "Other income" on your Form 1040 tax return; but as a sole proprietor, you report it as "Business income"—which you calculate by filling out a separate form, called Schedule C.

Why the different treatment? Because businesses are allowed to deduct certain business expenses, but hobbyists (with some very limited exceptions) are not.

At the federal level in the United States, the Internal Revenue Service (IRS) usually considers you a business if you operate with the intent of making a profit and you make a legitimate effort to make one. (For more details, visit the IRS website at www.irs.gov.)

If you do qualify as a business, and you keep your inventory carefully tracked, you can deduct your cost of goods sold (COGS) and general business expenses from your total business income. Your COGS are the direct costs of the finished goods that you actually sell. Your total COGS are the combined costs of all the items you sold during a tax period. As a crafter, most or all of your COGS will probably be for raw materials.

Other business expenses are deductible if the IRS considers them "ordinary and necessary" for your business. These can include costs of advertising, office supplies, professional services (such as hiring a bookkeeper), license fees, business use of your home or vehicle, and phone, mail, and Internet service charges. Specifically which expenses you can deduct depends on factors unique to your business. You should consult a bookkeeper or accountant if you have questions about them.

Hitting a Snag

Not all business expenses can be deducted for the tax year in which they were incurred; some must be capitalized, or deducted incrementally over a number of years. These "capital expenses" may include certain startup costs and purchases of business assets, such as furniture or machinery. If you think you may have capital expenses, ask a bookkeeper or accountant how to properly address them.

Self-Employment Tax

As a sole proprietor in the United States, you may be required to pay self-employment tax for Social Security and Medicare along with your federal income taxes. When this book was written, self-employment tax applied to any sole proprietor whose net business earnings exceeded $399 for the year. (Check with your accountant or the IRS to find out whether this rule has changed.)

Your self-employment tax liability is a percentage of your net profit, which you calculate using IRS Schedule SE. Depending on the laws in place when you file taxes, you may be allowed to deduct part of this tax from your total taxable income.

State and Local Business Taxes

The agency that issues your business license will likely require you to file a business tax return quarterly or annually. Business taxes are usually based on your gross revenue, which is your total revenue without subtracting any costs. However, in most jurisdictions, you must file a business tax return even if you make very few sales and do not owe taxes.

Your state or local government may also impose a tax on business personal property, which typically includes equipment such as machinery and retail fixtures. The tax is a percentage of the current value of these assets. As a crafter, you may not have any taxable personal property that you use exclusively for business purposes, but it's a good idea to talk to a bookkeeper or accountant to make sure.

Sales Tax

If your state has a sales tax and you hold a seller's permit, or if you sold in person in another state that has a sales tax during the tax year, you also need to submit a sales tax return. As with business taxes, your sales tax return might be due quarterly or annually.

Although taxation methods vary from state to state, many states require you to report your gross revenue for the tax period, subtract any exempt sales, and then apply the appropriate sales tax rate or rates (see the "Selling Secrets" under "Permanent Seller's Permit" earlier in this chapter), to the remaining sales. Be sure to file a return even if you made no sales subject to sales tax during the tax period.

Use Tax

Most U.S. states with a sales tax also require you to pay a use tax on purchases that you make from vendors in other states who do not charge you sales tax. Use tax applies to personal and business purchases, so you should report any out-of-state purchases of tools, equipment, or supplies for which you were not charged sales tax, but would have been if you had purchased them in-state. Depending on the rules in your state, you may be required to report these on your state income tax return or on a separate use tax return.

Reports That Help You File Taxes

By now you may be wondering exactly how to come up with the information you need to file your taxes properly—especially those pesky income taxes with their complex rules about expense deductions. That's where accounting and inventory reports come in.

Profit and Loss Reports

A profit and loss report, also called an income statement, is an accounting report that lists your sales, COGS, gross profit or loss (which is sales revenue minus COGS), expenses, and net profit or loss (which is gross profit or loss minus expenses). If you use business accounting software, you can use it to automatically generate this report for the tax period. Otherwise, you can submit your bookkeeping records to an accountant who can generate the report for you.

> **Bits and Pieces**
>
> In order for your profit and loss report to be useful, it's crucial that you keep your bookkeeping records up to date. When they are, completing tax returns usually isn't very difficult.

Inventory Reports

Notice that profit and loss reports include COGS, which you need to track in order to deduct them from your business income. And as I mentioned earlier, most of your COGS are probably from purchases of raw materials. But recall from Chapter 4 that raw materials and finished goods are tracked outside your standard bookkeeping records. This means you need a way to generate reports from your inventory records and integrate them with your business accounting system.

There are two ways to do this if you use accounting software. First, you can purchase a software upgrade that handles both bookkeeping and inventory management and adds COGS to your profit and loss report automatically. However, such upgrades are usually designed for larger manufacturers, and they can be expensive.

The second alternative is to track inventory separately with inventory tracking software or spreadsheets and use reports generated by that system in conjunction with your profit and loss report when you file taxes. We'll take a closer look at inventory tracking systems in Chapter 14.

Using a Federal Tax Identification Number

Federal tax identification numbers, also called Employer Identification Numbers or EINs, are numbers used by the IRS to identify businesses. Certain business entities and types, such as corporations and businesses with employees, are required to have EINs; however, sole proprietors without employees generally are not.

Even if you're not required to have an EIN, you may optionally get one to use in place of your Social Security number when you apply for business bank accounts and other services that require proof of business identity. Theoretically, this can reduce your exposure to potential identity theft. However, unless otherwise instructed by your accountant or the IRS, you should not use your EIN to file income taxes. Continue to file them as an individual using your social security number.

You can apply for an EIN free of charge on the IRS website or by submitting IRS Form SS-4.

Industry Regulations to Watch Out For

Some crafted goods and crafting procedures are specially regulated by local, state, or federal agencies. These industry-specific requirements are separate from any permits or licenses that may also be required. Some limit the types of raw materials you can use, and others require you to label goods in a very specific way.

An example is the California Lead-Containing Jewelry Law, which limits the amount of lead that any jewelry or jewelry component sold in California may contain. It applies to all jewelry but imposes its strictest limits on children's jewelry and body jewelry. Another is the U.S. Consumer Product Safety Improvement Act (CPSIA), which limits the use of lead and phthalates (a type of plasticizer) in all products intended for children.

SOLD   **Selling Secrets**

> As originally passed, the CPSIA imposed mandatory lead and phthalate laboratory testing and detailed, permanent labeling of children's products. However, the law was being reevaluated when this book was written, and its implications for crafters were unclear. I've included some resources in the Supplemental Appendix at www.craftychannels.com/resources to help you check its status.

The Importance of Compliance

So what's the point of all these rules and obligations, and why should you bother worrying about them? Most importantly, by staying legal you're playing a valuable role as a legitimate businessperson in your community. You're contributing to the economy and helping to protect people from harm.

But you should also know that if you fail to apply for the proper permits, pay correct taxes, or follow industry regulations, you may be hit with serious financial penalties—or, at the very worst, even criminal sanctions. That doesn't mean you should panic over the implications of any laws, but you should make every reasonable effort to comply with them.

The Least You Need to Know

◆ Take the time to learn which licenses and permits apply to your business, and get them.

◆ There are several types of taxes to report as a business, but they shouldn't be difficult to deal with if you keep your inventory records and accounting system up to date.

◆ Don't be afraid to hire a bookkeeper or accountant. It can save you lots of time and simplify your life as a more active craft seller.

◆ Always be on the lookout for industry-specific regulations that may limit the types of raw materials you can use or how you go about making your crafts.

Chapter  14

Growing Your Assets

In This Chapter

- ◆ Reevaluating your finished goods design options
- ◆ Buying in bulk and pricing for a profit
- ◆ Using inventory management software
- ◆ Selling your extra supplies

In this chapter, I'll help you take a more business-oriented approach toward planning out your finished goods inventory and selecting, buying, and tracking raw materials. As a follow-up to the previous chapter's discussion of income taxes, we'll also explore how you can use an inventory management system to determine your cost of goods sold (COGS).

Rethinking Your Finished Goods Inventory

Way back in Chapter 4, I introduced the concept of design options for your finished goods inventory. We looked at the differences between one-of-a-kind designs, limited editions, and stock designs as well as the pros and cons of premade and made-to-order goods. Now it's time to reevaluate the decisions you initially made about the composition of your inventory.

One-of-a-Kind vs. Production Work

First, you may need to reduce the number of one-of-a-kind designs in your inventory and replace them with stock designs or limited editions. That's because the extra time that one-of-a-kind designs require—for design, assembly, inventory tracking, and listing creation if you sell online—may impact your ability to make and maintain a profit. This is of special concern when you sell wholesale (see Chapter 18), where customers order in large quantities at discounted prices and you have a deadline for completing each order.

Switching from one-of-a-kind designs to limited editions and stock designs is sometimes referred to as moving into production work. By making multiple copies of the same design, you can purchase more raw materials in bulk, distribute the labor cost of each design among all the copies, and (optionally) focus on creating design collections rather than individual, unrelated items.

Design Collections

A design collection, sometimes called a product line, is a group of finished goods that shares certain style characteristics. You can design them to appeal to a particular type of customer or fulfill a specific need. As a more active seller, collections give you better control over your inventory and help you promote your business more effectively.

It's not necessary for the goods in a design collection to all be the same type, such as a collection of knitted socks or a collection of scarves. But they should share similar design features. For example, you might have a collection made up of socks, scarves, and other items that share a common color scheme.

To spark customer interest, you can schedule certain times of the year to introduce, or release, a new collection. Optionally, you can discontinue, or retire, past collections on those same dates. This gives customers two reasons to shop: they can be first in line for new items or snatch up old ones before they're discontinued.

Here are some more ways you can benefit from switching to design collections:

♦ **Better time management.**
Releasing collections on
a schedule makes it easier
to allocate time to design
work, promotion, and
selling.

♦ **Improved quality control.**
By focusing on a limited
number of similar designs,
you have a better chance of
discovering and addressing
quality issues.

Selling Secrets

Give your design
collections names that
communicate their style and
appeal to your target customers. For inspiration, browse
online shopping sites or thumb
through gift catalogs to see
how other artisans name their
own collections.

♦ **Ability to capitalize on trends.** You can create collections that
follow style trends and retire them before they fall completely out
of fashion.

♦ **Better branding.** Your
promotional campaigns can
focus on one collection at
a time, making it easier to
target subsets of customers.
Promoting one or two ongoing *signature collections* can
also set you apart from the
competition.

Term Tag

A **signature collection**
is a design collection
that is so unique that it distin-
guishes your work from other
crafters in your craft medium.

♦ **Building a more professional portfolio.** You can project a more
professional image by organizing your design portfolio into categories based on current and past collections.

Making the Most of Buying in Bulk

As a casual seller, you may have been unable to meet the minimum
order requirements for bulk discounts on raw materials and other supplies. But as a more active seller, you may need to meet them in order
to maintain a reasonable profit.

Understanding Bulk Purchase Requirements

Always read suppliers' bulk-discount policies carefully. You'll find that some offer a percentage off the total due for your entire order, even if the order contains many different types of items. Others offer discounts on a per-item basis, where you must purchase a bulk quantity of a single item in order to receive a discount.

Bits and Pieces

Some suppliers use the term "wholesale" when referring to bulk discounts that any customer can qualify for. Others use it to describe bulk discounts that are available only to business customers. They may request a copy of your seller's permit to verify that you are a business before processing your order.

Take this into consideration when planning out your inventory. If your finished goods are diverse designs that require many different types of raw materials, suppliers who offer only per-item discounts may not meet your needs. And even suppliers who allow you to mix items to qualify for a discount may not be of help unless you can find a single supplier that sells everything you need.

There are two ways to deal with these challenges as a more active seller. First, you can alter the makeup of your inventory so that more of your designs use the same raw materials. Selling by collection makes this doable without sacrificing creativity.

The second approach is to knowingly purchase more than you need and resell the extras later. Just keep in mind that selling supplies carries its own challenges and will require a larger time commitment than just selling crafts. We'll cover that in more detail toward the end of the chapter.

Using Inventory Management Software

In Chapter 4, I showed you how to use simple records to track raw materials and finished goods. But as your inventory grows, creating all of those records individually can eat up some serious time. And don't forget that you need to come up with inventory reports for your taxes, too.

You can save time by using inventory management software that is designed for businesses that have both raw materials and finished goods inventories. It may be a set of customized, integrated spreadsheets or a more sophisticated program that uses a database. See the Supplemental Appendix at www.craftychannels.com/resources for some examples.

Tracking COGS

In addition to tracking raw materials from the time you purchase them to their sale as finished goods, your inventory software should make it easy to generate a report that calculates your total COGS at the end of each tax period.

Bits and Pieces

Most inventory tracking software gives you the option of assigning a number, called an inventory number or SKU, to each raw material that you enter. Optionally, you can use these numbers to label the bins, bags, or compartments where you store the matching raw materials. This makes it easier to look up information about certain materials in your software application.

The IRS has specific rules for calculating both total COGS and the individual COGS for each item that you sell—and you need to make sure that your inventory software follows them. Start by checking to see how your software deals with fluctuating costs of raw materials over time.

Here's an example. Let's say that I placed two orders for the same type of beading wire during the course of the year. When I purchased the first batch, the cost was $15 per spool, but when I purchased the second, it had increased to $18 per spool. I need to know how my software deals with those two prices when it assigns COGS, and ensure that it complies with the IRS rules.

You may recall from Chapter 5 that, for purposes of estimating costs for pricing, we dealt with varying raw materials costs by averaging them. When this book was written, the IRS allowed a similar method, called "rolling average," for calculating COGS. However, the IRS also encouraged an alternative approach called First-In, First-Out (FIFO).

For my inventory software to apply FIFO, it would need to assign the $15-per-spool cost of wire to all the jewelry that I sold during the year, up to the time when that first spool would have run out. Then it would apply the $18-per-spool cost to any beading-wire jewelry that I sold beyond that, using an assumption that it contained the more recently purchased wire.

Now I know from reading my inventory software's manual that it uses the IRS-compliant rolling average method instead. However, because tax rules are subject to change, I need to stay on top of them. If I ever need or want to switch to the FIFO method, I'll have to purchase different software.

This is another area of tax law where a bookkeeper or accountant can be an invaluable source of information and advice.

Integrating Reports

As we saw in Chapter 13, your profit and loss report (the key accounting report that you use to report taxes) traditionally includes COGS. But when you track COGS in separate inventory management software, it will be missing from your profit and loss report.

That shouldn't be a problem as long as you and your accountant are aware that you track COGS separately. If you'd like to make your profit and loss report more complete, you can enter total COGS (from your inventory report) as a journal entry in your bookkeeping software.

> **Hitting a Snag**
>
> Don't forget that reports are just tools that help you make business decisions and prepare tax returns; they are not evidence of what really happened during the tax period. You must keep evidence of all your purchases and sales transactions, in the form of receipts and account statements, to support the data that you enter into your bookkeeping and inventory tracking software. You may need it if you're selected for a tax audit.

Reconciling Inventory

Even if you're careful about updating your inventory records, there can be discrepancies between them and the actual status of your inventory.

They can happen when, for instance, a piece of inventory is lost to theft, taken for personal use, or simply miscounted. Because discrepancies can affect your tax liability, it's a good idea to take an actual count of your physical inventory at the end of each tax period.

Most small business accounting software can help by generating a physical inventory worksheet that you use to record your counts and identify discrepancies. When you find a very minor discrepancy that you're unable to resolve quickly, you may decide to make a corrective entry in your bookkeeping records and move on. However, if you ever find a significant unresolved discrepancy, consult a bookkeeper or accountant to make sure you report your taxes accurately.

Inventory Software with Built-In Pricing

Some inventory software can be configured to apply pricing formulas to finished goods. This can help with initial price estimates, but remember that it's only part of the pricing process. As we saw in Chapter 5, you also need to consider market factors.

Selling Your Extra Supplies

Some crafters liquidate their extra, unused raw materials and other supplies by selling them to other crafters. It's a great way to keep inventory moving and money coming in, and it lowers the risk involved with buying supplies in bulk. However, you shouldn't jump into supply selling without giving serious thought to the complications it may bring to your business.

First, be prepared for your inventory tracking system to become even more complex. In addition to tracking raw materials in relation to your finished goods, you now must also track which raw materials are resold as merchandise. Merchandise has COGS (typically, the price you paid for them) just like finished goods do. Make sure that your inventory software is setup to include both types when it calculates total COGS for the tax period.

In addition, you may want or need to sell your supplies through different venues than your crafts. If you use a shopping site, that may mean opening a separate shop to keep your raw materials prices more private.

Bits and Pieces _____

In addition to their other uses, inventory numbers (SKUs) can come in handy when you sell raw materials as merchandise—especially if you sell online. You can use them to quickly find items when you assemble orders for shipment.

If you sell at craft shows, be aware that some may prohibit selling supplies and crafts at the same booth.

Finally, be prepared to develop and enforce a second set of business policies and practices for selling supplies. Because profit margins on supplies are notoriously low, you may decide to use more affordable shipping methods and simpler packaging and enforce stricter limits on returns.

The Least You Need to Know

◆ In order to make your business profitable, you may need to change the composition of your finished goods inventory. Consider focusing on design collections rather than individual pieces.

◆ Do what you can to take advantage of bulk discounts on raw materials and other supplies, which can lower your overall costs and help you make a profit.

◆ You can use inventory tracking software to save time and more easily calculate COGS, which you may be able to expense on your income tax return.

◆ There are benefits to selling leftover supplies, but make sure you're really ready before you begin.

15

Promotion for the More Active Seller

In This Chapter

- ◆ Using more advanced marketing materials and strategies
- ◆ Ways and places to advertise
- ◆ Promoting with other crafters
- ◆ Getting more public attention
- ◆ Finding out whether promotion works

Now that you're ready to make more sales, it's time to reassess your promotion techniques. What have you learned about your target customers since you first started selling? How are they responding to your business cards, newsletters, blog, and other promotional tools? Can you improve sales by updating your techniques or adopting new ones? In this chapter, we explore some ways that you can use promotion to achieve your goals as a more active seller. Resources for the materials and services covered are provided in the Supplemental Appendix at www. craftychannels.com/resources.

Using Brochures and Flyers

You can add to your arsenal of printed marketing materials by creating brochures and flyers. Brochures are usually tri-fold sheets of paper that introduce customers to your work. They're useful for handing out at sales venues and social events, and you can also mail them with shipped orders. Brochure templates are included with most word-processing programs.

Flyers normally contain less information than brochures. You can use them to make an announcement or invite shoppers to a special sales event. You can design them just about any way you'd like, hand them out like brochures, or mail them separately to past customers.

Announcing Strategic Sales and Discounts

Strategically plan times to announce sales or offer discounts on some or all of your crafts. You can schedule them for especially slow or busy times of the year or both. Make the announcements on your blog, in your newsletter, and on social networking websites. To track the effectiveness of sales and discounts, keep a record of the dates that you offer them. Later, you can review your bookkeeping records to measure your success.

> **SOLD** **Selling Secrets**
>
> Large businesses develop formal marketing plans to assess products, prices, target customers, competitors, and sales channels. You don't need this sort of lengthy document, but it's a good idea to keep the same factors in mind when you make promotion decisions.

Offering Coupons

You can encourage repeat sales by giving customers paper coupons with their orders or including coupons in your newsletter. If you have an e-mail list, you can also send coupons digitally for customers to print and use in person. If you sell online, you can provide coupon codes for customers to type in when they check out. Unfortunately, not all shopping sites give you the ability to automatically accept coupons. In that situation, the best you can do is instruct customers to enter their coupon code in the "Notes" section of the shopping cart and wait to pay until they receive a corrected invoice from you.

With all coupons, be sure to clearly state any expiration date, conditions, or limitations. As an example condition, you might require a minimum order amount; for a limitation, you might exclude certain items, such as clearance items or custom orders.

Advertising

Advertising can be an effective form of promotion—but only if it reaches your target customers and convinces them to make a purchase that they wouldn't otherwise make. Because most advertising isn't free, always set a weekly or monthly advertising budget and stick to it.

Where to Advertise

When deciding where to place an ad, think about your sales venue as well as your target customers. If you sell online, clickable online ads make sense. But if you sell in person, you should consider advertising in local print publications, such as newspapers and community newsletters. If you use online ads, limit them to websites with a local focus. Travel sites that showcase your town or city and sites managed by local clubs are potential candidates.

How to Advertise

An ad can be a simple line of text, a graphic design, or a photo. You can design your ads or hire a professional to design them for you. Look online for an independent designer who offers reasonable prices and understands craft marketing.

When you sign up to place an ad, the website or publication you apply to should provide submission guidelines. Typically, you can submit online ads in one of several universal image formats. Print ads can often be submitted in a standard digital image format for printing.

Selling Secrets

Online ads that contain graphics are often called banner ads. They're published in several standard sizes. Ad spots for larger banners are usually pricier than smaller banners on the same webpage. Banner placement also affects cost; banner spots near the top of a page generally cost more than spots at the bottom.

You can also collaborate with other craft sellers to make print advertising more affordable. This approach works like a co-op, where each member of an organized group contributes to the total cost of an ad space. The printed ad is then divided into several smaller ad spaces—one for each group member.

Search for collaborative advertising groups on crafting websites and shopping site forums. Because the available ad space is usually limited, try to find these opportunities well ahead of the time you'd like to advertise.

Bits and Pieces

Don't let worries about competition keep you from collaborating with other craft sellers. If you'd rather not promote work that's very similar to your own, seek out crafters who share your target customers but work in different mediums.

Online Key Word Advertising

Key word advertising, such as Google AdWords, is usually sold on a pay-per-click basis, where you're charged a fee each time someone clicks the link in your ad. Ads appear on the results pages for search engine key word searches. For example, if you purchase an ad for the key word "mosaics," it would appear (at least occasionally) when an Internet user searches for that term.

The key to making these programs worthwhile is to select key words and phrases that only your target customers are likely to search for. Let's say that you make mosaics primarily with found objects. Of all the people who search for "mosaics," only a handful might be interested in your particular style. You could narrow your results by purchasing ads for "found object mosaics" or even "alternative mosaics" or "unusual mosaics." This approach saves money because only the most promising prospects see—and potentially click—your ad.

Can You Advertise for Free?

Occasionally, you may find opportunities to advertise for free—especially online. Be very cautious about these. Don't sign up unless you're confident that there are no hidden strings attached.

A common form of free online advertising is link exchange, where a website owner agrees to place your link or ad on their site in return for you placing their ad on your site. At one time, these were useful for improving search engine ranking. However, the major search engine companies now penalize some sites that use link exchange. You can minimize this risk by exchanging links only with sites that are directly related to your crafts and that are not "link directories" of unrelated sites.

An even safer approach is to exchange banner ad space on your blog for ad space on someone else's. You can ask around in forums and on social networking sites to find other interested bloggers. To host an ad, you usually just need to paste a snippet of code into your blog that pulls up an advertiser's image and links back to their site.

Swaps and Giveaways

You can also collaborate with other crafters to swap promotional materials and sponsor promotional giveaways.

Promotional Swaps

With swaps, crafters exchange business cards, brochures, and fliers and distribute them to each other's customers. If you sell online, you can mail these materials in shipped orders. If you sell in person, you can keep them in stacks in your display area and give them away. As always, only join a group whose members share your target customers.

Promotional Giveaways

Some blogs and other websites hold regular product giveaways for their readers. You can sponsor a giveaway by sending photos of a product that you'd like to donate and agreeing to ship it to the blog owner or the prize winner. Although there are many legitimate promotional giveaways to choose from, you should always do some research before signing up for one. Make sure it has a good reputation and isn't a scam, especially if the blog owner asks that you ship the prize directly to them.

Another option is donating crafts to be sold, auctioned, or given away at charity events. It's a good idea to focus on local events—or, especially if you sell online, more distant events that are especially likely to attract your target customers.

If you craft small, less-expensive items, you can also consider donating them for use in gift (or "swag") bags that are distributed at larger business events. However, this is usually a better option for high-commitment sellers who can handle the expense of donating many items at once.

Looking for Press

Media attention can expose your crafts to lots of potential customers at little or no cost, and it's a more personal way of communicating than using ads. You don't need to be featured in a nationwide magazine or on a big television network to get results; some of the best opportunities are with local media and on the Internet.

Presenting Your Work

To have your work featured in print publications or on blogs and websites, you need to reach out to the people who manage them. The simplest approach is to send courteous e-mails introducing yourself and your work and expressing interest in being interviewed or featured. Point out a few of the benefits of your crafts, and attach one or more digital photos as examples.

If you'd like to get more serious, create a *media kit*. It can include your artist statement, photos and descriptions of your work (called your "portfolio"), and excerpts (or "clips") from articles or posts that featured your work in the past.

Term Tag

A **media kit** is a collection of materials that showcases your business and expresses your interest in receiving media attention.

High-commitment sellers sometimes hire public relations firms to design professional media kits, but you can make a basic version yourself. It can be completely online, as additional pages to your mini website (covered later in this chapter), or a series of color-printed pages that you enclose in presentation folders and mail to publishers and website owners.

Getting Reviewed

Depending on your craft medium, you might look for places to have your work reviewed. This often involves mailing a sample to a reviewer, who then writes about it. Because this usually requires giving a product away without any guarantee of receiving a review, it might not be a good option if your crafts are relatively pricey. As with promotional giveaways, always research a reviewer's reputation before sending him or her your product.

Giving Interviews

With interviews, an interviewer asks you a number of questions about yourself and your crafts. Interviews can be published as audio recordings, video recordings, or written articles and presented on television, online, or in print publications. When you do an interview for an article, you may be given a list of questions and asked to write out your answers, rather than giving them in person.

Interviews are great opportunities to tell interesting stories about your work, point out the unique benefits of your crafts, and let your target customers get to know you as a real person. Look for interview opportunities on crafting websites and blogs and with local newspapers and television stations.

Using Local Media

Local publications and television networks are always on the lookout for residents to feature. You can often catch their attention by simply notifying them that you're available. You might explain how you got into crafting, why you enjoy selling in the local community, or even how you decorated your home studio. Search the Internet or phone the publication or network to find out where you can mail a letter of introduction and your media kit, if you have one.

> **Hitting a Snag**
>
> Any media coverage can affect your privacy and may sometimes expose you to difficult people who wouldn't otherwise know that you exist. If this is a concern, try limiting your public exposure to more targeted audiences than those generally reached by television networks and newspapers.

After your initial introduction, you can keep in touch with local media by sending press releases (also called media releases). These are short articles that describe a change in your business, such as a new sales venue or design collection. You can find lots of free resources online for help writing and distributing press releases.

Expanding Your Internet Presence

In Chapter 8, I covered some ways that you can use the Internet for free promotion. Here are some options for taking online techniques to the next level.

Upgrading Your Blog

If you use a blog, consider updating its design. You can hire a graphic designer to create a blog template that better matches your color scheme and overall style. You might also add functionality to your blog by installing widgets, which are encoded tools that add interactive content such as photo galleries and favorites lists. Photo-sharing sites and shopping sites usually provide their own widgets that you can use for free.

Here are some more ideas:

- ◆ Sign up for a service such as Google Friend Connect to add social networking to your blog.

- ◆ Collaborate with other craft bloggers to write posts that link to one another's blogs.

- ◆ Create a blogroll, or a list of links to other craft blogs, and ask other bloggers to add your blog to theirs.

Creating a Mini Site

A mini site, sometimes called a business card site, is a single web page that you use solely for promotion. Because this kind of site doesn't need much functionality, you should be able to create one for free or sign up with a very low-cost website hosting service. Make sure the service you choose offers premade templates and the ability to create and update your page easily.

Use your mini site to introduce yourself and your crafts, provide links to your online sales venue, blog, and social networking sites, and to invite visitors to join your e-mail list. Most e-mail list services provide a snippet of code that you can paste onto a web page to create an automatic sign-up form. This is especially useful if you use an online shopping site that doesn't offer its own e-mail list function. You can also post photos of your work on your mini site and link to your photo-sharing account. Don't forget to add the URL of your mini site to your next round of business cards.

Sharing More Digital Photos

Many craft sellers use a photo-sharing site, such as Flickr, to display photos of their work. To use one, you set up an account and follow the directions for uploading digital photos from your computer. People can find your photos by running key word searches on the site's main page. As with shopping sites, you can create tags for photos to help people find them. You can also join photo-sharing groups to have your photos included with photos of work by other crafters.

Photo-sharing sites typically allow you to set copyright permissions that dictate how other people can use your photos. At the strictest level, you can reserve all rights, which means that no one has the right to copy your image and post it on their own website or blog. Alternatively, you can allow your photos to be used for only noncommercial purposes—or you can permit them to be used for any reason at all.

Consider permitting at least some of your photos to be used in blog posts with attribution, meaning that the bloggers must identify the photos as yours and link back to your photo-sharing page. This makes it easier for bloggers to write about your work and give you free promotion.

> **Bits and Pieces**
>
> Some high-commitment sellers produce look books or catalogs of their work to present to resellers. These are printed materials that contain photos of designs in a particular line or collection. You can use a similar approach to create online photo galleries that showcase various categories of your work.

Assessing Your Progress

Do your best to track your promotion efforts so that you know when to change or improve them. How you track them depends on which promotion methods you use.

Tracking Online Promotion

If you sell online, you can use a free web analytics service such as Google Analytics (www.google.com/analytics/) to track how many people visit your online shop—and, more importantly, how they got there. For example, if someone clicks to your site from a blog post, the analytics report will show the date and time that the click occurred and identify the blog's URL as the referring site.

An increase in visits to your sales venue is generally a good thing, because visiting is the first step in making a sale. But you also need to track how many visitors actually make a purchase. This often requires comparing your web analytics reports with your sales records over a period of time. You can't always determine exactly where each sale originated, but you should get an idea whether your online promotion tactics are effective.

Tracking Print Promotion

Tracking the effectiveness of print promotion can be more challenging. A standard approach is to try one promotion tactic at a time, and check your bookkeeping records for its impact on sales. Although this is a good start, it isn't a perfect solution because it's hard to know whether your promotion tactic was the real reason for an increase in sales.

For instance, let's say you run an ad in a local newspaper for an upcoming trunk show. The show has lots of visitors and is a success. The following month, you hold another trunk show at the same location, but you don't run the ad. If your sales are lower for the second show, how can you be sure the ad made the difference? Lots of other factors can impact sales, including economic conditions, weather, and competition from another local event that diverts shoppers' attention.

Here are some ways you can sleuth for answers to these questions:

◆ **Ask your customers.** When you make a sale, courteously inquire how the customer heard about your sales event.

◆ **Attach special offers to ads.** Offer a discount or inexpensive free gift to customers who mention or present your ad when they make a purchase. Or, promise a coupon or gift to anyone who presents the ad, whether or not they make a purchase.

◆ **Make the most of your mailing list sign-up sheet.** Add a field to your newsletter sign-up sheet for subscribers to jot down how they heard about you.

◆ **Use a guest book.** Keep a guest book in your display area where visitors can enter their first name, the city or town they live in, and how they heard about you. Consider offering an inexpensive free gift for anyone who makes an entry.

Your goal is to subtly glean as much information as you can from people who visit your display, whether or not they make a purchase. Even if you can't determine precisely how effective a given promotion tactic is, over time you'll get a feel for what works.

The Least You Need to Know

- Improving your promotion strategies can help you make the sales you need as a more active seller.

- If you decide to advertise, be sure to target your customers and watch your budget.

- With a little effort, you can have your work featured in print and online publications or on local television.

- Learn from experience, and be prepared to change your approach when you don't see positive results.

Part 5

Sales Venues for the More Active Seller

This final part of this book covers some additional sales venues that you can explore, now that you have a more refined inventory, a robust bookkeeping and inventory tracking system, and a little experience under your belt.

First, I'll take you through the general process of setting up your own e-commerce website. It's completely optional, but you just might find it worthwhile. We'll then examine craft shows, with a focus on how they differ from trunk shows and sales parties. We'll wrap up with a look at how you can start selling wholesale to resellers and make use of some wholesale alternatives.

Chapter 16

Selling on Your Own Website

In This Chapter

- ◆ Deciding whether a standalone site is right for you
- ◆ Getting started by finding a shopping cart
- ◆ Using a template to design your site
- ◆ Hosting your site and securing a domain name
- ◆ Operating your website and getting it noticed

Until now, I've talked mostly about using shopping sites as online sales venues. But what about setting up an independent e-commerce site of your own? Autonomy can be worthwhile if you have the time—plus a little patience—to devote to website management.

In this chapter, we'll explore how you can start a website and generally what it takes to keep it going. We won't revisit the basics of selling online, such as how to select sales categories, write product descriptions, and upload photos. (Review Chapter 9 if you need a refresher on those topics.) Resources for the products and services covered in this chapter are listed in the Supplemental Appendix at www.craftychannels.com/resources.

The Pros and Cons of Website Independence

Before we get into the details of how to establish a website, let's weigh the pros and cons of having one.

Website Challenges

Standalone websites are more time consuming and complicated to manage than shops on online shopping sites. Here are the three primary reasons why:

♦ Something always needs tweaking, from design elements that don't align properly to text that needs updating.

♦ You often need to install and maintain your own applications, such as shopping carts and search functions.

♦ In order to make sales, you must do even more promotion than you would on a shopping site.

Term Tag

Hosting services, also called hosts, provide space on Internet servers for websites. You should wait to sign up for one until you understand the hosting requirements of your shopping cart.

But there are other things to worry about, too. You need to find a *hosting service* with a reliable web server, devise a way to upload files and photos, and learn how to make adjustments to your site over time. If you accept credit cards, you may also need access to a secure web server to protect customers from identity theft.

Website Benefits

The greatest benefit of operating your own site is that it features only your wares; you don't compete for site visitors' attention. Another perk is having the freedom to design your site entirely to your specifications, which helps you communicate your brand identity. You're also free to add extra content to your site, making it more likely to receive positive attention.

Selecting a Shopping Cart

The first step in creating your site is deciding which shopping cart application to use. The benefit of a shopping cart is that it allows customers to purchase and pay for multiple items at once. Most carts also add applicable shipping fees and sales tax to each order.

Here are the three categories of carts from which you can choose, along with some information to help you select one.

Payment-Processor–Hosted Carts

The simplest shopping carts are hosted by online payment processors such as PayPal (www.paypal.com) and PayMate (www.paymate.com). To use one, you paste a link onto your site for each item you have for sale. Customers can use these links to place items into a shopping cart. Depending on which payment processor you use, customers may or may not need to sign in before they can checkout.

The biggest downside of these carts is that they're usually branded with the payment processor's name, logo, and color scheme. (Although you might be able to add your own logo to the shopping cart pages, this may require access to a secure server, which we'll talk more about soon.) You also have limited control over how many pages your customers must click through during checkout and what information they're asked to provide.

On the other hand, because these carts are hosted on the payment processor's server, you don't need to worry about keeping credit card numbers secure, and you're typically not responsible for troubleshooting if the cart malfunctions.

Carts You Install

To have a fully customized shopping cart, you typically need to install one on your hosting service's web server. (We'll cover installation later in the chapter.)

Sometimes these carts are part of larger e-commerce packages that also create catalog pages for your site. One popular example is Zen Cart (www.zen-cart.com), an open-source program that you can download for free.

E-Commerce Platforms with Built-In Carts

A third option is to sign up with a service that provides an entirely preinstalled e-commerce package, or platform. These include Yahoo! Merchant Solutions, ProStores, and Big Cartel (see the Supplemental Appendix at www.craftychannels.com/resources). They are rarely free, and how much you pay for them depends on the functionality you need. Most charge a recurring flat fee, and some also take a percentage of each sale. They're usually relatively easy to set up, and they come with their own hosting.

> **Bits and Pieces**
>
> Many shopping carts have some inventory management functionality. However, they only track the finished goods that you list on your website; they do not track raw materials or calculate COGS (see Chapter 13) and therefore they cannot replace your inventory management software.

Creating a Website from Scratch

The traditional way to create a website involves writing code into files and then using a File Transfer Protocol (FTP) program to upload them to the Internet. Basic FTP programs are available online for free. Some examples are SmartFTP (www.smartftp.com) and CoffeeCup Free FTP (www.coffeecup.com/free-ftp/). Your hosting service gives you the information you need to configure your FTP program so that it can connect to your site.

The standard code used for web pages is called HyperText Markup Language (HTML). You can purchase web design software, such as Dreamweaver or FrontPage, which helps you use it without knowing much about the code itself. However, it's still pretty challenging to create a functioning e-commerce site on your own. Consider using a website template instead.

Finding a Website Template

Templates are precoded web pages you can customize with your own colors, fonts, artwork, and photos. How you go about doing that depends on the type of template you use. Some must be edited before you upload them to your site. Others can be accessed online through an administration, or "admin," page. When you shop for a template, be aware that some are more difficult to customize than others.

Most e-commerce platforms and packages have one or more built-in templates. You can also purchase one from a third-party template vendor or hire a web designer to make one for you. Ask around in the crafting community for referrals.

Selling Secrets

It's possible to use a payment-processor–hosted shopping cart (such as PayPal) with a blog template. You switch into HTML mode in your blog interface and paste the links into your posts. However, you need to make sure that your blog host's terms and conditions allow for commercial use; they may not if your service is free.

Selecting a Hosting Service

Unless you use a preinstalled e-commerce platform (see the section "E-Commerce Platforms with Built-In Carts" earlier in this chapter), you need to select a hosting service for your site. Payment-processor–hosted carts can work with just about any hosting service, but carts you install yourself have specific requirements.

Basic Hosting Requirements

First, your host's server usually must be configured to process a particular version of a scripting language called Hypertext Preprocessor, or PHP. This allows your shopping cart to follow sets of operational instructions. Second, it must have a database utility, such as MySQL. This is where all the information for your listings is stored.

Any reputable hosting service's website will indicate whether it has these functionalities and in which versions. However, the easiest way to find a compatible host is to check your shopping cart service's website. It should provide a list of recommended, or "certified," hosts. Some may even install your shopping cart for you.

Free Hosting?

Call me an ogre, but I don't recommend that you select a hosting service that purports to be free. Free hosting is usually limited in functionality and less reliable than paid hosting (which means that your site might not always be accessible), and free hosts often place advertising on your site that annoys and distracts visitors. You should be able to find an affordable hosting plan that meets your requirements and provides better service.

Security Requirements

If you accept credit cards or collect other private information from site visitors, you may need access to a secure (SSL) web server (see the "Accepting Credit Cards Through Your Site" section later in this chapter). Pages hosted on a secure server usually have "https," rather than "http," in their URLs. Although most of your site can reside on an unsecured server, your shopping cart checkout pages require the added protection.

Registering a Domain Name

Hosting is not the same as having a domain name. When you first purchase hosting, your URL is usually a directory on your hosting service's domain. For example, if I purchase hosting for Chetti Designs

from HostGator, my default URL may be something like
http://chettidesigns.hostgator.com. In order to use my own URL,
http://www.chettidesigns.com/, I must register that domain with a
service called a domain registrar.

If your hosting company is also a domain registrar, you can register
your domain through them. Otherwise, you need a third-party registrar, such as Dotster or Network
Solutions. Start by visiting the
registrar's site and running a
search for the domain name you're
interested in. If it's available, you
have the option of registering it
for an annual fee.

Your hosting company should
give you instructions for setting
up your new domain to work
with your website. Typically, you
need to paste your host's "name
server" into a form on the domain
registar's website.

Hitting a Snag

Be very careful not to
allow your domain name
registration to expire. Always
pay its renewal fee on time.
If your domain does expire,
not only will customers have
a hard time finding your site,
but your domain may also be
registered by an unscrupulous
company that aims to steal
your website traffic.

Setting Up Domain E-Mail

Once you register a domain name, you can set up an e-mail account
that uses it, often for a small fee. For example, if I set up an e-mail
account for www.chettidesigns.com, I could use chris@chettidesigns.com
instead of the chettidesigns@gmail.com that I use with my free e-mail
account.

Your registrar should give you the option of adding e-mail service to
your domain registration account. Just log in and follow the directions
for adding e-mail. You can then either use a free online e-mail application to access your e-mail or configure an application on your computer
to download it.

Getting Your Site Up and Running

With a preinstalled e-commerce platform, you can log in to an admin area on the provider's website and follow the directions for setting up and activating your site. Otherwise, you'll need to get things going yourself. Just how you do that depends on the type of cart and template you use.

Installing a Shopping Cart

If you select a shopping cart or e-commerce package that you need to install, it should come with installation instructions. You'll probably begin by opening some files and making minor changes to the code. You can do this using a free program called a text editor. Some examples are HTML-Kit (www.chami.com/html-kit/) and Alleycode (www.alleycode.com/).

Then you'll need to use an FTP program to upload the shopping cart files to your host's server. Your shopping cart instructions should explain how to do this in detail.

There may be several more steps to complete after your upload, such as copying files or changing some files' security permissions. Your hosting company should provide instructions for these tasks.

Finally, you should be able to access your site's admin area, or control panel, by logging in to a special web page on your host's server.

Installing a Template

If you use a template that needs to be installed, it too should arrive with installation instructions. Check to see whether you need to make edits before or after uploading and how you can make those edits. It may be possible to make them through an online admin area. If you must make edits by opening the file on your computer, be prepared to upload it again to the Internet any time you make changes.

Configuring Your Site

Once your shopping cart and template are correctly installed, you can access your shopping cart or e-commerce package admin area and change its settings to reflect how you want your site to function. At a minimum, this involves entering your business name, sales tax and shipping information, and the payment methods you accept.

Bits and Pieces

Many shopping carts and e-commerce packages start with very basic functionality, which you can improve by installing add-ons or modules. For example, some carts have an optional module for shipping profiles similar to the ones you might use on shopping sites (see Chapter 9).

Next, follow the instructions for creating new pages and pasting in your policies. It's also a good idea to create pages for your biography (bio) and contact information.

With the rest of your site configured, you can begin creating sales listings. As always, carefully follow the instructions provided by your e-commerce package or template. For each listing, you'll need to paste in an item description and enter a price and shipping information, just as you would on a shopping site.

Accepting Credit Cards Through Your Site

Unless you use a payment-processor–hosted shopping cart, you need to configure your cart to accept credit cards. The method you use depends on how you plan to handle credit card processing. If you use your cart to collect credit card numbers that you process later, your cart must be configured to store them on a secure server.

Another option is to connect your shopping cart directly to your merchant account so that card numbers are processed automatically. This requires an application called a payment gateway, which may be offered as an extra service by your merchant account provider. Although a payment gateway usually comes with a fee, it saves you from needing to pay for access to a secure server through your host.

Slogging Through the Finishing Touches

It can take some time to get your site looking and operating exactly as you'd like, especially if you do your own installations and design work. Try to be patient, and hire an indie web designer if you need help.

As part of the process, be sure to add a link to your blog on your new site as well as an invitation to sign up for your e-mail list. Most e-mail list service providers offer a snippet of code that you can paste in to create a sign-up form.

Also, do what you can to make your site friendly to search engines. We'll talk more about that later in the "Attracting Visitors" section.

Using Your Website

Place a test order or two to make sure your site is functioning properly. Once it is, you're ready to roll. Your site may already be "live," or publicly accessible via the Internet. If not, access your admin area and follow the instructions to open for business.

Receiving Orders

Customers can browse your online catalog and checkout to place orders, much like they would on a shopping site. Unlike most shopping and auction sites, however, you can require that your customers make payment immediately when they check out.

Depending on how your shopping cart is configured, you may receive an e-mail notification each time you receive an order, or you may need to log in to your admin area to check for orders manually. (In that case, set a daily schedule for checking.) Be sure to keep your customers updated on the status of their orders, just as you would on a shopping site.

Hitting a Snag

Websites can look and function differently on different web browsers, such as Internet Explorer and Firefox. You can check your site for cross-browser compatibility by downloading recent versions of the most popular browsers and using each to visit your site, or by signing up for a browser compatibility–checking service.

Gauging Customer Satisfaction

Although your site probably won't be configured to receive customer feedback ratings such as those on shopping and auction sites, you can take other measures to find out how customers feel about their orders.

One option is to create an online questionnaire that you send to each customer a week or two after shipping an order. You can even create one for free using a service like Google Docs. Search online for tutorials on how to set one up.

At a minimum, be sure to send every customer a follow-up e-mail to confirm receipt of their order and ask whether they have any questions.

Making Site Backups

When you have your own site, it's important to make regular backup copies of all its pages and data. Both your host and shopping cart provider should offer backup instructions. Set a backup schedule that's convenient and minimizes the amount of data you'll lose if something goes drastically wrong with your site. Keep your backup copies in a special folder on your computer, or transfer them to a storage device (such as a thumb drive).

Planning for a Vacation

Devise a way to notify site visitors whenever you're unable to process orders for more than a couple days. Shopping sites usually give you the option of temporarily closing your shop for vacation, but your own site may not. At a minimum, plan to post a vacation notice throughout your site—and, if possible, set up an e-mail auto-responder to remind customers when you'll return.

Attracting Visitors

Unfortunately, merely creating a website is not enough to attract the customers you'll need to make it worthwhile. Be prepared to work hard to encourage your target customers to visit your site. And be patient—it might take many months before your site starts to catch people's attention.

Getting Searched

First, make sure your website is coded and configured in a way that allows search engines to index it properly. Here are three initial tasks to focus on:

◆ Enter a site title, description, and key words into the corresponding fields on your web pages (these are called meta tags).

◆ Set up logical, key word–focused site navigation (or menu) links.

◆ Create useful content, such as tips articles and stories about your crafts.

You can learn more about these tactics on your shopping cart provider's website or on the information pages of popular search engines.

If you use a preinstalled e-commerce platform, check the provider's help pages to learn how they optimize their templates for search engines. Follow any guidelines they provide for making and keeping your site searchable.

It may take some time for your site to become indexed in search engines. You can find tips for improving its search engine ranking in books devoted to website design and maintenance. You can also hire a search engine optimization firm to help out, but beware of potentially unscrupulous firms that promise more than they can reasonably deliver.

Getting Links

Unless your site does very well in search engines, most of its visitors will probably arrive by clicking a link on another website. For this reason, it's usually valuable to have links pointing to your site from other sites that attract your target customers. However, you must be careful about how you go about acquiring inbound links. Submitting your link to directory sites that search engines classify as "link farms" can actually lower your ranking in search results.

Safer options include placing your link in your signature when you comment on forum or blog posts and purchasing advertising on other sites. For more information about those tactics, review Chapters 8 and 15.

Bits and Pieces

The measure of how many quality sites link to your website is called link popularity. In addition to giving people opportunities to click into your site, inbound links can actually improve your ranking in some search engines.

Keeping It Fresh

Make a habit of occasionally adding new content to your site, such as articles about your crafting techniques, photos and stories from craft shows, product size charts, and other resources that visitors may find helpful. This increases your odds of getting found in web searches, encourages repeat visitors, and gives you interesting material to link to in your e-mail newsletters or on social networking sites.

The Least You Need to Know

- ◆ As a crafter, having your own e-commerce site is purely optional. If it's more than you'd like to take on, use an online shopping site instead.

- ◆ If you decide to create your own site, start by selecting a shopping cart and then finding a hosting service that meets your needs.

- ◆ You can register a domain name through a domain registrar, which may or may not be the same company that provides your shopping cart or hosting.

- ◆ Be prepared to work hard to publicize your site, and don't expect it to become popular overnight.

Chapter 17

Selling at Craft Shows

In This Chapter

- ◆ Selecting a craft show
- ◆ Understanding and assessing vendor fees
- ◆ How to sign up for a show
- ◆ What to do before and after a show

Organized craft shows, fairs, festivals, and markets—where you set up a booth and sell alongside many other crafters—can be lucrative sales venues. The trick is to select the right show, arrive fully prepared, and learn from each show experience.

Many of the tasks involved in preparing for and selling at a craft show are the same as for trunk shows. In this chapter, we'll focus on the differences between the two. Before doing your first craft show, reread Chapter 11 for important tips on setting up a display, accepting payment, processing sales, and interacting with shoppers.

Finding the Right Shows

You can find local craft shows in craft show directories, which are available in print and online. In some cities, the local chamber of commerce also maintains lists of events that accept vendors. You'll find that most shows are recurring in that they're held at about the same time each month or year.

Craft Shows vs. Trade Shows

As you begin your craft show search, be aware of the difference between craft shows and trade shows. Craft shows are open to the public and target retail customers; trade shows are typically private shows open only to wholesale customers and their representatives. Unless you transition into crafting full time and focus on selling wholesale, you'll probably want to stick with craft shows.

Attending as a Visitor

It's a good idea to visit a recurring show before applying to it as a vendor. Take note of the types of people you see attending and how they spend their time. Are they busily shopping, or are other attractions diverting their attention? Do the shoppers match your target customer profile?

Bits and Pieces

Ask for advice about particular shows from other members of the crafting community. Local crafters are the most helpful, but when they're not available, post your questions online.

Also, assess the show vendors. Are their wares in your price range? Are they of similar or complementary style? Is there much competition among vendors who share your craft medium?

As you browse around, don't be afraid to strike up conversations with vendors. Smile and ask how their sales have been, whether they've attended the show before, and whether they plan to attend again.

Requesting Information

Once you've identified a potential show, contact its organizer or visit its website for answers to the following questions:

- **Is the show limited to handmade crafts?** It's frustrating to compete against vendors who sell mass-produced goods or handicrafts made in countries with different economies. Look for shows that cater to sellers who make their own crafts.

- **How many visitors are expected to attend?** You may make more sales at larger shows, but smaller shows are less intimidating—especially when you're just starting out.

- **How many vendors are expected to attend?** To be a success, a show needs a winning ratio of visitors to vendors. If there are too many vendors for the number of visitors, your sales may suffer.

- **Is there a cap on the number of vendors that will attend?** If not, the show might have less draw than a more restricted show; however, its fees might be more reasonable, too. Also, check whether there are caps on the number of vendors in each craft category, which can reduce competition.

- **What is the show organizer's marketing strategy?** Find out how much the show is advertised and where.

- **Is there access to electricity?** Learn whether electric outlets are available for plugging in lights and any electronics that you want to use at the show.

- **How are booth spaces allocated?** If booth spaces are filled on a first-come, first-served basis, you'll have less control over how accessible your booth is to shoppers—and your arrival at the show may be extra stressful.

- **What are the vendor space rules?** Some shows limit the style and types of tents or table coverings that vendors can use. Dimensions, design, and placement of signs and banners may also be restricted.

Taken together, these answers should give you an idea of what to expect from a show and whether you really want to take it on.

Vendor Fees

Vendor fees, the fees that most show organizers charge for a show, are always a factor when deciding whether to apply. Here are the different types of vendor fees you're most likely to encounter:

- **Booth fee.** This is typically a flat fee that covers the rental of your booth or table space. Many shows have more than one size of space from which to choose.

- **Application fee.** Sometimes called an entry fee, this is a flat fee that you pay when you apply for a show. It's often separate from the booth fee and covers the labor involved in processing your application.

- **Jury fee.** A jury fee pays for someone to review your application to a *juried craft show*.

Term Tag

With a **juried craft show,** all vendor applications are reviewed by a panel or committee, and only a limited number of vendors are accepted.

- **Commission.** When a show organizer takes a commission, the organizer receives a set percentage of your total show sales. Some shows charge both a booth fee and a commission (watch out for these—they can be pricey).

- **Insurance fee.** Show organizers sometimes give vendors the option of buying in to a cooperative liability insurance policy. Refer to Chapter 12 for a refresher on insurance.

- **Amenity fee.** This is typically an optional fee that you may need to pay for access to an electrical outlet for your booth.

Many organizers require you to pay a deposit on fees when you apply for a show or when your application is accepted. Read show applications carefully to find out whether, and under what conditions, deposits are refundable.

When Is a Fee Too High?

Craft show fees can range from less than $20 to more than $1,000, with most falling within the $50 to $100 range. As a more active seller, you should generally avoid any fee that is likely to keep you from making a profit. Your minimum goal is to make enough sales to more than cover all your costs—including vendor fees, costs of getting to the show, your own labor, and your COGS for the items you sell at the show.

The Five-to-Ten-Times Rule

Over time, most craft show vendors discover that they make a reasonable profit at a show if their gross sales revenue is between at least 5 and 10 times the total vendor fee. I call this the "five-to-ten-times rule."

Although it may not apply perfectly to your situation, this rule provides a good starting point for determining whether a show will be worthwhile. As you become more experienced, you can refine it to better match your needs.

Here's my approach for applying the five-to-ten-times rule:

1. **Multiply the total vendor fee by five and by ten.** The revenue that you generate at the show needs to fall, at a minimum, somewhere between those two numbers.

2. **Divide each number by your average sales price.** The result is your estimated sales volume, or the number of items that you need to sell at the show.

3. **Decide whether you have enough inventory to potentially make that many sales.** If not, the show is probably too expensive.

4. **Consider other factors that may affect sales.** Even if you bring lots of inventory, it may not sell as well as you'd like.

5. **Consider cumulative show expenses.** Costs of travel, lodging, and meals, combined with the show fee, may make it too expensive overall.

The Rule in Action

Here's an example. Let's say that all my jewelry is priced similarly, for an average price per piece of about $50. The show that I'm considering charges a total of $200 in vendor fees. It's a local show, so I won't have to worry about long-distance travel or lodging expenses.

First, I calculate the estimated range of minimum sales revenue that I need to generate at the show:

$5 \times \$200 = \$1,000$

$10 \times \$200 = \$2,000$

My range is $1,000 to $2,000.

Next, I use my average price to translate that into minimum sales volume:

$\$1,000 / \$50 = 20$ pieces

$\$2,000 / \$50 = 40$ pieces

This means I would probably need to sell between 20 and 40 pieces of jewelry to make the $200 fee worth my while.

Now I need to identify any factors that might reduce my ability to make adequate sales at this show. I may ask myself:

- Will this show attract the types of shoppers who are truly interested in my crafts?

- If I've attended similar shows in the past, how well did my crafts sell?

- Will there be much competition from other vendors in my craft medium?

- Does the show take place before the holidays, when sales are typically higher, or in early summer, when they may be low?

Evaluating Show Commissions

The five-to-ten-times rule is useful only for shows with flat fees. If a show charges a commission instead, check your pricing methodology (see Chapter 5) and determine whether you can accommodate the commission and still make a profit on each item you sell.

Applying for a Show

Many shows have websites where you can download a printable application or apply online. With others, you need to call an information number and request that an application be mailed to you.

Keep in mind that most shows begin accepting applications months in advance and have application deadlines. Apply early, and don't forget to include payment for any fees that are due up front.

Filling Out the Application

The most important part of a show application is the vendor statement, where you're asked to describe your work. This is your opportunity to explain why you'll be a benefit to the show. Focus on what's unique about your crafts and why they're a good fit.

You may also be asked to provide photos of your booth or display. If you already have some show experience, use photos from a previous show; otherwise, use a shot that you took during your trial-run setup (which we'll get to shortly).

For juried shows, you must also provide high-quality photos of several pieces of your best work. Traditionally, these needed to be slides, but some shows now accept digital or print photos. If you don't have the necessary equipment to take professional-looking jury photos, hire a photographer to take them for you.

Other items that you may need for your application include:

♦ **A copy of your resale permit or your resale number.**
Remember that this needs to be for the jurisdiction where the show is held. As I mentioned in Chapter 13, most counties and cities offer temporary seller permits for shows.

◆ **Insurance certificate.** Some shows require you to provide an insurance certificate, which proves that you have liability coverage for the show. Revisit Chapter 12 to read about liability coverage.

◆ **Booth, table, or display specifications.** You may be asked for the dimensions of your booth and display area. Be sure to take and record measurements during your trial run-through.

It may also be worthwhile to include an information card or brochure with applications that you submit by mail. Your artist biography (bio), additional photos of your work, and press mentions can also help your application get noticed.

Selecting Booth Size, Location, and Extras

For shows where you have a choice of booth size, you typically make that selection by checking a box on the application. The location you select may or may not be guaranteed. You may also be asked whether you'd like any special amenities, such as electricity.

Bits and Pieces _____

Booth location is almost always important. Try to select a spot that exposes you to lots of shoppers, such as a corner space or one near food vendors. When possible, avoid areas that visitors are likely to visit last, when they're tired and the excitement of craft shopping begins to fade.

Understanding Show Rules

By submitting an application, you agree to comply with the show's vendor rules. They may limit the time you can be absent from your booth, designate setup and tear-down times, and control the size and type of tent, table coverings, and banners you use.

Also watch for payment method requirements. Some shows require you to either accept credit cards or allow your customers to pay at a payment booth provided by the show organizers. In that case, the show keeps a percentage of each credit card transaction they process for you.

Waiting for a Response

After submitting your application, the best you can do is begin initial preparations for the show and wait patiently. Show organizers should provide a time frame for notifying vendors of their application status. If you don't hear back within that time, politely call them to check.

With juried shows, many applicants may receive rejection letters. If you're not accepted into a particular show, don't take it personally. Reevaluate your application materials and look for anything you can improve. If you can spruce up your vendor statement or photos, do so now so that you're ready for the next try.

Preparing for a Craft Show

The way you get ready for a craft show is similar to how you prepare for a trunk show or sales party, with the possible exceptions that you may need to bring more inventory and design a more elaborate display.

How Much Inventory Do You Need?

For shows with flat fees, you can refer back to the five-to-ten-times rule to estimate how much inventory to bring: take your projected sales volume from that calculation and multiply it by two or three. This helps ensure that you have a large enough selection to satisfy shoppers.

Recall from my earlier example that I probably need to sell at least 20 to 40 pieces of jewelry at my show. Here's how I can use that figure to estimate how much inventory to bring:

20 pieces × 2 = 40 pieces

40 pieces × 3 = 120 pieces

So I'll plan to bring a minimum of 40 to 120 pieces of jewelry to the show. Because that's a pretty broad range, exactly how much I bring depends on what I have available, how much I can fit into my vehicle along with my equipment and supplies, and how large of a selection I think I'll need for this show.

I also need to decide whether these goods will all be unique designs or whether some will be copies. Either is acceptable as long as I offer a reasonable variety. And there's no need to display my entire inventory at once. I may choose to keep some items behind my table and bring them out later to replace items that are sold or just to change my display.

For a show that charges a commission instead of a flat fee, use your best judgment about how much inventory to bring. Or, guess how many items will sell, and plan to bring at least one and a half to two times that amount.

What Else to Bring

Unlike trunk shows and sales parties, craft shows often run from morning until late afternoon or early evening. Do your best to bring whatever supplies you may need to avoid having to abandon your booth to hunt something down.

It's a good idea to make a general supplies kit that you take to every show. It can include things such as hair care accessories, facial tissues, lip balm, hand wipes, medications, contact lens solution, and first-aid supplies. Also plan to bring drinks and food. You might also arrange for someone to bring you lunch or dinner at the show.

And don't forget all your basic selling-in-person supplies, such as your cash box or apron, pens, receipts, and equipment for processing credit cards as well as your display props, table covers, and lights. If you use electricity, bring some extension cords for plugging into outlets.

Hitting a Snag

Don't worry about bringing decorative packaging materials to most craft shows. Shoppers rarely expect more than a simple bag for carrying their purchases home. You can use organza drawstring bags if your goods are small enough or paper shopping bags stamped with your seller name.

Designing Your Booth

This is one of the most important (and fun) parts of getting ready for a show. For both outdoor and indoor shows, you need one or more display tables and a chair or two. Select tables that are easy to transport, carry, and erect—but make sure they're also sturdy. A flimsy card table can make you look unprofessional (and, even worse, might blow over in the wind).

Especially if you do outdoor shows, you also need a show tent or canopy. Look for a professional model that's designed for craft vendors, rather than one intended for recreational use. Professional vendor tents are typically sturdier, easier to set up and take down, and include special features such as side zippers that give you lots of configuration options. They're also white in color, as required by many craft show organizers.

Your tent should also be water resistant and leak proof in case you get caught in the rain. Watch out for cheaper models that allow rain water to puddle on their roofs, which can lead to a tent collapse.

Your tent needs to be weighted or staked down at its outside edges to protect it from blowing over or scooting. You can make your own bean bag–style weights or purchase them along with tie-down stakes from your tent vendor.

You may also decide to bring a portable floor covering for your booth, such as carpet or wood tiles. But choose these wisely—avoid any loose edges or folds that visitors may trip over.

Getting a Banner

Most shows allow you to display a banner with your business name or a description of your crafts. You can order a plastic banner from larger office supply stores and printing shops or hire an indie textiles designer to make one for you from fabric. Tie your banner to the upper front edge of your tent or hang it across the front of your table.

The Trial-Run Setup

Just as you would for a trunk show, run through your entire booth and display setup plan at home before attending a show. Designate a space with the same dimensions as your booth space, and experiment with configurations until you discover something you like. Then tear everything down and load it into your vehicle. Make sure it fits and is easily accessible.

Last, remove everything from your vehicle and set up your booth once again, this time using a timer. If you run into any problems, they're likely to be worse at the show—so take time to address them now. You may want to photograph or sketch your final configuration to use as a map when you set up at the show.

Safety First

During your trial run, check your booth carefully for any potential safety hazards. If you plan to use electricity, you need to guard against fire and electric shock. If you have tall displays or breakable items such as mirrors, devise a way to keep them from tipping or falling. Some show tent suppliers offer hooks and straps for this purpose.

Other Ways to Get Ready

Here are some more general tips for preparing for a craft show:

- ◆ Write about the show in your newsletter, mention it online, and send announcements to people on your mailing list.

- ◆ Choose show attire that's stylish but also comfortable. Consider packing work gloves and athletic shoes to wear when setting up and tearing down your booth.

- ◆ Don't forget to bring cash for making change, just as you would for a trunk show.

- ◆ Buy a cable lock for securing your cash box to your tent or table (or use a cash apron instead).

- Try to plan your display to discourage shoplifting, which is more common at craft shows than trunk shows.

- Make sure your craft show business policies are up to date. (For an example, see "Knantucket Knits Show Policies" at www.craftychannels.com/show_policies.)

Recruiting Help

Although it's possible to work a craft show by yourself, bringing a helper gives you more freedom to temporarily leave your booth and is generally more fun than manning a booth alone. Look for a family member or friend who's willing to help.

When you do need to work alone, try to have someone visit you at scheduled times so you can take bathroom breaks and, ideally, get help setting up and tearing down your booth.

Bits and Pieces

Some shows allow more than one crafter to apply together to share a booth. This is a great option if you have a relatively small inventory and a crafty friend who targets the same types of customers. It also conveniently solves the challenge of finding someone to watch your booth when you need to take a break.

After the Show

The day after a show ends, process any credit cards and deposit any checks that you received. Within a week, be sure to update your books and count your till and inventory just as you would for a trunk show.

Consider designating a notebook or computer file for jotting down your thoughts about each show. They'll come in handy if you attend the same show again or consider applying for a similar show.

The Least You Need to Know

- ◆ You need to research many different aspects of a show to determine whether it's a good match.

- ◆ To decide whether a show's vendor fee is too high, estimate how many sales you must make to justify it and whether you really can make them.

- ◆ Understand and follow all show rules, which should be outlined on the application.

- ◆ Practice loading, unloading, setting up, and tearing down your booth before your first craft show.

- ◆ Get your bookkeeping records, money, and inventory in order after a craft show just as you would after a trunk show.

Chapter 18

Selling Wholesale

In This Chapter

- ◆ Establishing wholesale policies
- ◆ A closer look at wholesale prices
- ◆ Where and how to sell wholesale
- ◆ Using reseller's venues to make sales

Selling to resellers is much different from selling directly to retail customers. You need to price your wares lower while still making a profit, set distinct policies, and adhere to buyers' schedules. But selling wholesale also has its advantages, especially if your ultimate goal is to become a full-time craft seller. If you're successful, you can eventually give up selling retail and focus more of your time on crafting.

Setting Wholesale Policies

Before you begin searching for resellers, take time to develop a separate set of policies and practices for wholesale orders. Write down your wholesale policies in a clear, organized manner for presenting to potential customers. (See "Knantucket Knits Wholesale Terms" at www.craftychannels.com/show_policies for an example.)

Here's a look at what your policies might include.

Business Customer Requirements

Some crafters prefer to offer wholesale discounts only to legitimate, licensed resellers. This limits the possibility that retail customers will group up to take advantage of your discounts (if that idea bothers you), and it may help you avoid unsavory resellers that can tarnish your reputation.

To limit your wholesale customers to real businesses, you can require them to provide a copy of their resale certificate (or at least their resale number) before they place an order. Look up resale certificates in a state database online, or call the issuing agency to confirm their validity.

Offering Tax Exempt Sales

When you sell to a reseller in your own state and that state has a sales tax, you can usually avoid charging sales tax by having in-state wholesale customers fill out certificates of resale. You can obtain a blank certificate from the agency that issues your resale permit.

Keep copies of the certificates of resale that you receive. You'll need to report your tax exempt sales at tax time and provide the certificates to back them up if you're audited.

Payment Terms

Whether you accept credit card payment for wholesale orders may depend on how much the processing fees will impact your profit. Profit margins on wholesale orders can be low to begin with, and most merchant account providers take between 2 and 4 percent of each sale. Remember that most merchant account terms of service prohibit charging extra for credit card orders to make up for these fees.

Wholesale orders may also be more prone to credit card fraud than smaller retail orders. This is a concern particularly with international customers. As a rule, you should never ship a wholesale order outside your own country until you receive cleared payment that is not subject to a potential chargeback. Most merchant account providers allow chargebacks for up to six months or more after a sale.

Once you decide which payment methods to accept, think about when payment should be due. If a wholesale order is made up entirely of goods that are finished and ready to ship, you can require immediate payment. If you need to craft more items before the order is ready, you can compensate for the delay by charging 50 percent of the total due up front and the remaining 50 percent when the order is ready to ship.

Bits and Pieces

Sometimes, a wholesale customer may request Collect on Delivery (COD), where payment is due at the time the shipment is delivered. That payment is collected on your behalf by the carrier. Whether you agree to COD is up to you, but remember that it always carries the risk that the buyer will refuse (and effectively cancel) his or her order when it arrives.

Some serious wholesale craft sellers extend credit to customers with whom they've developed a business relationship. This puts the craft seller in the role of debt collector, which I don't recommend unless you plan to sell crafts full time.

Turnaround Time

Your turnaround time sets your deadline for completing a wholesale order. It's a good idea to set turnaround times on a case-by-case basis, depending on an order's composition and size. Be sure to give yourself enough time to acquire raw materials and craft any goods that you don't have immediately available.

Wholesale Returns and Exchanges

Your wholesale return policy should grant customers a reasonable period of time to inspect their orders and contact you about any missing, damaged, or unacceptable items. However, you should limit that return period and strictly enforce it.

The risk is that some resellers will ask to return goods that they are unable to sell quickly at retail—which is usually unfair to you as a wholesaler. As a general rule, you should only offer wholesale discounts to customers who assume the responsibility of reselling them.

If you do decide to accept wholesale returns, clearly state the circumstances under which you'll accept them, and consider offering exchanges rather than refunds.

Shipping

Decide whether to include the costs of shipping wholesale orders in your prices (essentially treating them as overhead) or whether to charge separate shipping fees. If you charge a fee, plan to define it as the actual cost of shipping—rather than a flat fee—because wholesale orders can vary considerably in size and weight. Always purchase shipping insurance for wholesale orders. It's also a good idea to require signature confirmation of delivery.

Other Terms and Conditions

Optionally, you can add other terms to your wholesale policies, such as a reminder that you retain the copyright to your designs or a requirement that your goods be resold with their original hang tags in place. If you sell your crafts online, however, be aware that resellers may prefer that you not include your website address on tags, labels, or cards.

Also, decide whether you are willing to provide display props or retail packaging for your goods. You should only offer them for free if your wholesale prices adequately cover their costs.

Finally, if you regularly sell one-of-a-kind items at retail, consider whether it really makes sense to sell them wholesale. The added time for designing and perfecting techniques can tip the scales against making a profit when you sell bulk orders at significant discounts.

Working with Wholesale Prices

Once your wholesale policies are in place, you should address how best to communicate prices to potential wholesale customers. You also need to consider how your wholesale prices may affect your retail prices going forward. (To review wholesale pricing generally, see Chapter 5.)

Using Price Sheets

How you disclose your wholesale prices depends on your overall business model. If you also sell retail, you can offer a simple percentage discount for bulk purchases. Alternatively, you can provide resellers with a price sheet that lists the wholesale price of each of your products.

Hitting a Snag

Never provide wholesale customers with unrealistic retail prices. It is misleading, and potentially illegal, to suggest a retail price that is unreasonably high based on your knowledge and experience. Also avoid suggesting prices that are above what you sell the same items for at retail.

Price sheets are most commonly used by serious sellers who sell wholesale exclusively, but you also can use them to project a more professional image. They're most effective when organized by collection; you can "release" a new price sheet whenever you introduce a collection, and distribute that sheet to prospective buyers.

In addition to listing wholesale prices, price sheets can include descriptions and photos or sketches of your products. Optionally, you can also provide suggested retail prices to subtly emphasize the value of your wholesale discounts.

Should You Keep Wholesale Prices Confidential?

Keeping wholesale prices confidential (between you and your wholesale customers) is another issue to consider, particularly when you sell online. Although disclosing wholesale prices on your website arguably makes it easier for resellers to place orders, some resellers frown on the practice. They prefer to shield their retail customers, and their competition, from knowing the prices they pay.

For this reason, you should at least consider keeping your wholesale prices private—especially if you want to attract more serious wholesale accounts. Instead of listing prices or bulk discounts on your site, provide a way for potential wholesale customers to request them.

Balancing Wholesale with Retail

Selling goods at wholesale prices can impact how you sell them at retail. Most importantly, you need to avoid undercutting your wholesale customers' retail prices—especially if you target the same customers (which is almost always the case when you sell online, because customers can access your site from just about anywhere).

Some crafters avoid this issue by selling wholesale exclusively—at least when it comes to selling online. Another approach is to make a practice or policy of never undercutting your wholesale customers. This means being aware of your goods' resale prices and limiting the retail discounts that you offer through sales and coupons.

Finding Wholesale Customers

With your wholesale policies and prices finalized, you're now ready to head out and find some resellers. As always, focus on venues that attract your target customers. Check other crafters' websites for lists of the stores to which they sell. You can also gain access to reseller directories by signing up with local or national craft societies and clubs.

Here are the categories that wholesale customers typically fall into and how you can pursue each one.

Brick-and-Mortar Venues

Good brick-and-mortar bets typically include gift shops, boutiques, and art or craft galleries. With most of these businesses, at least one person is in charge of purchasing inventory. You'll need to talk to that person and convince him or her that your crafts will interest the business's retail customers. How you do that depends on your comfort level and style. Most crafters use an approach similar to this one:

1. **Make initial contact.** If possible, find the name of the owner or buyer by researching city business listings or simply by calling the business and asking (briefly explain that you're an artisan looking for new wholesale accounts). Mail them a brochure (and, optionally, a price sheet). Include a note offering to stop by with samples of your work.

2. **Follow up.** Make a follow-up phone call and courteously ask whether the owner or buyer has had a chance to review your materials. Again, offer to stop by with samples.

3. **Visit, discuss, and listen.** If you're invited to meet with your contact, act professionally and respect their time constraints. Describe your crafting style and process, and mention whether you're available to hold a trunk show or "meet the artist" event. This can be a great way to test the market and to promote your line if you get the account. Then make a point of really listening: learn what the business's needs are, and identify how your crafts can help to fulfill them.

If a business is not accepting new vendors or orders in your craft medium, thank your contact nicely and invite him or her to call you if circumstances change. Avoid being pushy. Most businesses that sell crafts make a limited profit and must be highly selective about which merchandise they buy and when.

Retail Catalogs and Websites

Occasionally, you may find a reseller who publishes a catalog or operates a website. These businesses often have premade information packages or applications for potential vendors. Follow their guidelines for submitting your work, and do your best to demonstrate why your crafts are a great fit for their venue.

Only apply to a resale catalog or website if you're confident that you can meet its terms. For instance, many catalogs require you to produce hundreds of copies of the same design.

Sales Reps

Serious craft sellers sometimes hire sales representatives, or "reps," to seek out wholesale customers. For payment, reps take a percentage of each sale—often up to 30 percent—as commission.

Because they work on commission, good reps are selective about the crafters they take on. If you become a full-time crafter, you may find that the effort and cost involved with finding and using a rep is worthwhile. You might even discover one willing to market your wares at lucrative trade shows.

Negotiating with Resellers

Some wholesale customers may wish to negotiate different terms than you state in your standard policies. How much you're willing to negotiate often depends on how important a particular wholesale order is for your business.

Selling Secrets

Many online forums, including those on shopping sites, have static discussion threads devoted to selling wholesale. Use them to search for answers to your questions, and ask the advice of more experienced sellers.

When you're just starting out and struggling to make sales, you understandably might be more open to less-favorable terms. Over time, if the demand for your products increases, you can become more selective.

Accepting and Processing a Wholesale Order

When a reseller offers to purchase your crafts, don't let your excitement detract you from the tasks still at hand. Here's what those tasks typically include.

Finalizing the Agreement

When you and your wholesale customer reach an agreement on terms, you should find a way to record that agreement. The formal approach is to write up a sales contract that you both sign, date, and keep copies of.

For more casual agreements, you may decide to simply exchange e-mails that contain order details. Be sure to copy yourself on any e-mails you send to your customer, and print copies of all exchanged e-mails for your files.

If you sell in person to a reseller who does not use e-mail, at a minimum you should include your agreed-upon terms on both copies of the sales receipt.

Completing the Order

If you have crafting to do in order to fill a wholesale order, get started as soon as possible. Missing your turnaround deadline looks unprofessional and can harm your reputation. Moreover, it gives your customer a reason to back out of the agreement—resulting in potential conflict.

If you get behind, consider enlisting the help of family or friends. Although they might not have your skills, they can probably take on some simple tasks. If necessary, set up a production line in your dining room or garage, and get busy.

Serious wholesale sellers sometimes hire temporary employees to help fill large orders. If you want to go this route, however, speak with a business attorney first. There are specific laws that apply to employment, even when it's only temporary.

Packaging the Order

Package your wholesale orders with utmost care, especially if your goods are breakable. You can make a good impression by wrapping each item in tissue paper that matches your marketing color scheme. For smaller items, consider placing each in its own paper, plastic, or organza bag, tied at the top with a ribbon. Include a thank-you card and a personal note with each shipment, and invite the customer to contact you with any questions.

Bits and Pieces

Inform wholesale customers about any special care that your goods require. A common example is sterling silver, which may need frequent polishing. If possible, make it easy for customers to perform this maintenance while your goods are on display. For example, with silver jewelry you might include a free polishing cloth with each order.

Getting Feedback

Once your goods are available for sale at the reseller's venue, check in with your contact from time to time and see how they're selling. If sales are slow, see whether you can help. You might volunteer to rearrange the display, help with promotion, or schedule a free crafting demonstration for the reseller's customers.

Also ask resellers whether any of your designs sell particularly well. It may help you decide what to focus on for future orders and might even give you ideas for new collections.

Selling Wholesale Through Your Website

In the previous sections in this chapter, I focused on a traditional approach to selling wholesale, where you essentially pound the pavement to find customers. But you can also offer wholesale discounts through your own e-commerce website. If you sell retail on the same site, make a separate section for wholesale. Optionally, you can protect it with a password and request resellers to contact you for access (this is another option for keeping wholesale prices private).

Alternatives to Selling Wholesale

When you're just starting out, you might receive more offers for what I call "alternative selling arrangements" than for true wholesale orders. The three most common types are consignment sales, arts and crafts co-ops, and drop shipping.

Selling on Consignment

With consignment, the operator of a retail venue—called the consignee—agrees to display your goods along with their own merchandise. They essentially borrow your crafts rather than purchasing them. When an item sells, the consignee keeps a percentage of the sales price.

Consignment percentages, or commissions, often range between 20 and 50 percent of retail. (Keep this in mind when you set your prices.) Consignment also has the following disadvantages:

- There is no guarantee that your goods will sell. And even if they do, you receive payment for them incrementally over time, rather than up front.

- While your goods are on consignment, they're unavailable to sell anywhere else—potentially resulting in missed sale opportunities.

- Your goods may not be properly cared for while on consignment and then returned to you unsold in poor condition.

- Conflicts may arise between you and the consignee if goods are lost, stolen, or damaged while on consignment.

- The consignee may go out of business, making it difficult or impossible to recover your goods.

If you decide to sell on consignment despite these risks, think about how you might negotiate to limit them. Will the consignee agree to display your goods prominently, promote them, and maintain them? Will they hand out your business cards and display your artist biography? Will their insurance cover your goods' damage or theft?

You should also make sure that the consignee has a system for recording which of your goods have sold and how much they sold for. Less-experienced consignees may ask you for a blank form or spreadsheet for recording this information. Schedule a regular time, such as once or twice per month, for collecting your consignees' sales data and your payments for any sales.

Be sure to find a way to track which goods are on consignment at a given time. You can set up a spreadsheet for consignment tracking or purchase a premade one. If you routinely switch out consignment goods to keep the selection looking fresh, be sure to update your consignment records accordingly.

Co-Ops

Arts and crafts co-ops are typically set up as galleries where member artisans offer their wares for sale together. The co-op accepts payment on your behalf and keeps a percentage commission. Many co-ops also charge monthly membership fees or require each member to volunteer to work at the co-op sales desk.

To join a co-op, you need to submit an application and be accepted by the current members. You may also need to schedule an interview or attend a meeting to introduce yourself and your work. Because co-ops are owned and operated by the artists and crafters themselves, they're typically less risky than traditional consignment venues.

Drop Shipping

Some websites and catalogs may offer to drop-ship your goods rather than purchase them. Typically, they agree to create listings for your goods on their sites, and when a customer makes a purchase, they collect payment and notify you. You are then responsible for packaging the order and shipping it to the customer. At some point, often after confirmation that the customer received his or her order, the drop-shipper sends you payment for the item less a commission.

Keep in mind that drop shipping has risks for both you and the drop-shipper: you may be required to ship goods before receiving payment, and the drop-shipper must rely on you to ship on time.

The Least You Need to Know

- ◆ Before you start selling wholesale, establish wholesale business policies that are separate from your retail policies.

- ◆ In order to find wholesale customers, you usually need to seek them out, market your wares effectively, and be open to negotiation.

- ◆ There are alternatives to selling wholesale that, although often less desirable, can still be useful ways to make sales.

Sample Policies and Practices

This appendix provides examples of how you can write your business policies for online and wholesale sales channels. (For examples of policies that you might display at a craft show, see www.craftychannels.com/show_policies.) Toward the end, you'll also find a sample list of business practices. You can use all these samples as rough templates, but be sure to update them in accordance with your own policy and practice decisions. See Chapter 7 for help.

Sample Policies for Selling Online

Use a word-processing program when you write your online selling policies so that you can easily paste them into web pages.

Knantucket Knits Online Shop Policies

Payment

I accept credit cards and other forms of online payment through PayPal. I also accept personal checks and money orders; however, please note that checks can take up to two weeks to clear, resulting in a delay in shipping. Payment is due within seven business days of placing your order.

Shipping and Handling

I currently ship anywhere within the United States, Canada, Mexico, and Europe. Combined shipping and handling fees are shown in each listing. If you purchase more than one item, shipping and handling is the fee for the heaviest item plus 50¢ for each additional item.

Shipment is by U.S. Postal Service First Class or Priority Mail, depending on package weight. I typically ship within three days after payment clears. Insurance is automatically included for U.S. deliveries but not for international shipments. Please note that I cannot be responsible for uninsured packages. If you live outside the United States and would like insurance, please contact me for a quote before placing your order.

Sales Tax

Orders shipped within California are charged a sales tax of 8.75 percent. If you pay with a check or money order, please be sure to include sales tax in your payment.

Returns

You may return a noncustom order for a refund or exchange within 14 days. Returns must arrive in their original condition. Refunds are for the purchase price less shipping and are made through PayPal if you paid with PayPal or by check if you mailed your payment. Please let me know whether you'd prefer to exchange your order for a different item.

I normally cannot accept returns of custom orders, but if you have any questions about one, please contact me.

Caring for Your Knitwear

My knitwear should last for years with proper care. Please follow the care instructions included with your order, and contact me anytime with questions.

Custom Orders

I'm available to make a special scarf just for you. Please contact me with as many details as possible about what you have in mind, and I'll get back to you soon with ideas.

Note: These policies are subject to change. Any updates will appear on this web page.

Notice that I included care information in these policies. Even though I don't offer a quality guarantee, I want customers to know that I'm available if they run into problems. This also gives me the flexibility to respond on a case-by-case basis.

Sample Policies for Selling Wholesale

Although some resellers will want to negotiate additional terms, it's a good idea to present them with some standard baseline policies.

Knantucket Knits Wholesale Terms

Wholesale Discounts

Discounts are based on the number of items purchased, according to the following table:

Number of Items Ordered	Discount
5 to 10	20 percent
11 to 25	30 percent
26 or more	40 percent

Payment

◆ Payment may be made by check or money order.

◆ One half of the order total is due upon order placement, and the remainder is due when the complete order is ready to ship.

Shipping

◆ Unless otherwise agreed, shipment is by UPS Ground with signature required upon delivery.

◆ The actual cost of shipping is included in the total due.

Other Terms

◆ Please notify me within three days of receiving your order if any items are missing or not as described.

◆ You may return your order in full, in its original condition, within five business days of receipt for a full refund less a 10 percent restocking fee. I cannot accept later returns.

◆ I retain the copyright to all Knantucket Knits knitwear.

Sample Business Practices

As with the sample policies, the following practices are examples but not necessarily recommendations; be sure to adopt practices that work for you.

Payment Practices

When a customer pays in person with a check:

◆ Ensure that the address on the check matches the address on the customer's driver's license or identification card.

◆ Write the customer's full name, address, phone number, and driver's license or identification card number on your (the seller's) copy of the sales receipt.

If payment for an online order is late:

◆ Notify the customer and remind them of the payment deadline.

◆ If there is no response within three more days, cancel the order.

◆ If the customer responds and asks for more time, agree to no more than a one-week extension before canceling the order.

◆ Leave negative feedback on a shopping site only if the customer ignores all contact attempts.

If a customer sends a form of payment that I don't normally accept:

- For a domestic order that doesn't seem suspicious, accept payment but notify the customer that I cannot accept this method in the future.

- If the order is international (with a higher risk of fraud), refuse the payment and ask for repayment in an acceptable form.

- If the customer rejects that request, apologize and cancel the order.

If an online customer mistakenly fails to pay sales tax:

- When sale tax is minimal, ignore the mistake and treat tax as being included in the purchase price.

- If sales tax is substantial, notify the customer and courteously ask for a follow-up payment. Extend the payment deadline within reason.

Shipping Practices

If a customer requests shipment to a nonmatching address:

- Refuse to ship to that address but offer to ship to the address that is linked to the customer's credit card or payment processing account.

- If the customer rejects that offer, apologize and cancel the order.

If a customer requests shipment to a location where I don't normally ship:

- Apologize and refuse to ship to that location.

- If the customer does not provide a suitable substitute address, cancel the order.

If a customer notifies me that their shipped order never arrived:

- If the package shipped with delivery confirmation or tracking, check the number to confirm nonreceipt.

- If the delivery confirmation or tracking check indicates that the package was delivered, courteously notify the customer.

- If there's no evidence of delivery and the package was insured, begin the insurance claim process.

- If there's no evidence of delivery and no insurance, apologize to the customer and consider offering a partial refund, depending on the circumstances.

If a customer notifies me that their order was damaged in the mail:

- For an insured package, begin the insurance claim process.

- For an uninsured package, ask for more details to determine the reason for the damage.

- Consider accepting a return for repair, exchange, or refund on a case-by-case basis.

If an international customer asks me to write "gift" or "sample" on a customs form:

- Courteously refuse and offer the customer the option of either accepting accurate customs information or canceling the order.

General Customer Service Practices

I will notify all online customers when:

- Payment is received.

- Payment clears.

- An order ships.

If a customer asks for a modification to their order after receiving it:

- Agree to perform a feasible modification for the cost of labor and materials.

- If the modification makes the item less durable, refuse to perform it and offer a refund or exchange instead.

If an online customer claims that their order is not as I described it:

- ◆ Allow the customer to return the order, and agree to cover return postage if my description was inaccurate.

- ◆ If my description was accurate, allow the customer to return the item but do not refund or cover shipping costs.

If a customer asks to return a custom order:

- ◆ Consider this on a case-by-case basis, but refuse returns of items that are unlikely to resell.

If a customer from an in-person sales venue requests a return:

- ◆ Ask them to meet me at an upcoming sales event and extend the return deadline as necessary.

- ◆ If I don't have an upcoming event, ask them to make the return by mail and reimburse the customer for return shipping on a case-by-case basis.

Index

J–K–L

M

Q-R

S

T